Conscious Evolution:
Mythology in Action

Conscious Evolution:

Mythology in Action

Dr. Maurice Turmel

Marble, NC USA

2014

Copyright © 2014 Word Branch Publishing
All rights reserved. This book or any portion thereof may not be reproduced or used in any manner whatsoever without the express written permission of the publisher except for the use of brief quotations in a book review.
This is a work of fiction. Names, characters, businesses, places, events and incidents are either the products of the author's imagination or used in a fictitious manner. Any resemblance to actual persons, living or dead, or actual events is purely coincidental.

Second Edition 2014
Printed in Charleston, SC USA

Cover illustration © 2014 Julian Norwood

Permission can be obtained for re-use of portions of material by writing to the address below. Some permission requests can be granted free of charge, others carry a fee.

Word Branch Publishing
PO Box 41
Marble, NC 28905

http://wordbranch.com
catherine@wordbranch.com

 Library of Congress Control Number: On file

ISBN-13: 978-0692258446
ISBN-10:0692258442

To All Inhabitants
of
Planet Earth
Awakening Now
"Your Time is at Hand"

Foreword

Conscious Evolution – Mythology in Action is the non-fiction followup to my novel *The Voice – A Mythological Guide to Mankind's Ascension*. This mythical story traces the adventures of a group of novices who have discovered that their sole purpose is to train for and participate in the consciousness raising of Earth's human inhabitants. They learn that this active evolutionary process consists of moving from 3rd dimensional density consciousness – the consciousness of separation – to 5th dimensional unity consciousness – the consciousness of oneness - as decreed by Heaven to occur at this particular moment in the Earth's history.

With unity consciousness there is no "us" versus "them". There is only "us" and we are One, in unity with all life and the Divine Creator.

The current book delves into mythology, psychology and our recently reclaimed spirituality to explain what our characters in The Voice are going through, and what we, as this planet's human family, are facing within ourselves.

Both of these books serve as a road map to the truth that lies within every individual soul now walking this earth in a human body. The access point to this inner reference of truth is The Heart.

This very real shift in human consciousness is now urging all of us to look within. Both The Voice and Conscious Evolution show us how.

Table of Contents

Contemplating Change 2
Author's Introduction 3
Feeling Welcome 13
Introduction from *The Voice* 14
    Evolving 19
1 – The Hero Myth 20
    Opening Your Heart 25
2 – A Hero's Welcome 26
    Self & Ego 32
3 – Heroes and Heroines 33
    Growing 38
4 – Life as Movie and Myth 40
    Asking for Help 47
5 – How We Lost Our Way 48
    Fear 52
6 – The Big Sleep 53
    Secrets 61
7 – Conscious Evolution 62
    Grace and Glory 68

8 – The Force 69
   Receiving 74

9 – Beyond Healing 76
   Paying Attention 81

10 – The Road to Discovery 82
   You Are Enough 88

11 – The Circle 89
   Friendship 92

12 – The Voice 93
   Companions 100

13 – A New World 101
   Touch 107

14 – Coming Home 108
   Trajectory 112

15 – Once Upon a Time 114

16 – A Roadmap for Ascension 117
   Wanderings 124

17 - Journaling 125
   Opposites 129

18 – Childhood 130

19 - Our Feeling State 136

20 – Adolescence	140
Passion & Purpose	148
21 – Meet the Players	150
22 - Making Choices	169
23 - The Dialogues	174
Transformation	184
24 – Destination Ascension	187
25 - Getting the Juices Flowing	191
26 – Getting Connected	194
Message From the Ethereal	200
27 – Wrap Up and Final Word from Guidance	203
Bonus Chapter from The Voice	208

Conscious Evolution

Part I

Mythology

Dr. Maurice Turmel

Contemplating Change

It seems beyond all understanding at times, what it is we have to learn about ourselves. Complex creatures we are, running around this world like chickens with our heads cut off. Are we sure this is what we want to do? Are we certain we want to construct our lives in such a fashion as to waste energy every time we turn around? There must be a better way. Let's take a closer look, shall we?

It's not that we actually know any better, at least not until we see a different way presented to us. Then we're confronted with the possibility that life could be different. We could perhaps slow down a pace or two. We could pick up on one another's thoughts and see how life looks from that perspective. We could liquidate our morality for a day and adopt another's, like a new pair of shoes, and see if they fit.

There are many antidotes to this fast pace we live. Is it necessary? Will the Earth spin faster if we move more quickly? Aren't there places in the world where the population moves at a measured pace, taking time to smell the flowers, as they say? Let's see if this break neck pace is really necessary. Let's put on another coat and see how we feel. It's a better world for us when we try a few different things.

Don't let this fast pace drop you like an old shoe on the side of the road. These people speeding by are not caring about you right now. To them, you're just a blur. Care for your Self. See if that pace you adopted has to carry on. If not, then give yourself a break. Maybe there's a better way.

Author's Introduction

The Voice moves through me and speaks to me in my thoughts, my dreams and my poetic expressions. It lies at the core of my being and surfaces as I call it forward and allow it to surface. Twenty years ago I began to channel, or what I thought was channeling at the time. Today I know The Voice as my Higher Self, my guidance and my spiritual support system. What I once thought of as channeling has simply revealed itself as "connection" - something millions of us humans are now capable of and quite comfortable with. The Voice, my Higher Self, inspired this work and its evolution. It is only fitting that this part of me, this connection, have a say in introducing the current work that We, once again, brought forth together.

Today there is a growing need to examine our systems of thought and communication. We are witness to an information explosion. Never before has there been such a plethora of relevant, and perhaps, not so relevant, information available on every subject imaginable. Most of us cannot even begin to fathom the depths of this seemingly inexhaustible supply. So how do we process what is coming at us now? What will be there for us in the future? There has to be a way to sort through this landslide of facts and fiction, to go over each piece and determine for ourselves its inherent validity and relevance to our lives.

In each epoch in mankind's history there were major transition points that affected all of humanity. These were marked by chaos, fear and upheaval, all related to a convulsive present and an indeterminate future. The Agricultural Revolution came about when we, as a species, stopped wandering and gathering and started cultivating fields and growing our own food. The Industrial Revolution began with the vast process of mechanizing our work. In each case, an old way was leaving, while a new way was being born. During these transition phases, chaos and upheaval were the signs of the times. Many current writers, including this author, are certain that this is the case now, with what we identify today as the Information Revolution and the coming shift in consciousness already begun as we engage the Age of Aquarius.

In previous periods of transition, some sense of order had to be derived from the chaos that was at hand. Some way of making sense of the whole unfolding process was required and led to adaptations that helped define the age. It wasn't a question of not living through it, because such radical changes were already upon the population. It was always a matter of how to adapt and temper this impact on the day to day lives of ordinary people.

"History repeats itself," we are often told until a particular lesson is learned. What is history trying to teach us right now? Are we unprepared for the great leap forward that is now upon us? In part, this may be true. But, what else? I draw sustenance from an old adage that says when a person is ready, what he or she needs, will come along. In other words, when a person commits to a course of action he or she will open their selves to what the Universe has to deliver.

What does that mean? The process of awakening and evolution is, from this perspective, a personal one. What is next on the horizon becomes visible after a current pressing challenge has been fully addressed. In so much as we are capable of mastering a given challenge, we shall be prompted to undertake it. This suggests that evolution doesn't necessarily take us where we want to go, but most certainly where we need to go. Once again, that fact doesn't become visible until its time arrives through the undulating process of change and transformation.

Evolution, here, is not solely a matter of biology, but more so a matter of personal awareness. What are the experiences of my life, as opposed to the experiences of your life? At some level we share a commonality of information and experiences. Those that underlie the world's religions are shared perceptions. Those that underlie our essential humanness are also shared. Do these perceptions and experiences hold any truth or not? And on what can we base our collective experience and subsequent testimony? After sorting through an enormity of facts, what do we rely on for a meaningful interpretation? How do we know when any interpretation is valid?

In our distant past, we had mythology to guide us through transitional and volatile times. Myths and their companions, parables, were guideposts; signs along the path that helped explain aspects of our human plight and imminent challenges. Myths and parables, as teaching tools, were developed to advance the human species, as individuals and nations, into and through the next stage of their evolution. Myths and parables were the shared information and processing tools of the times because, essentially, few individuals knew how to read. Since so little of the population enjoyed that privilege, there evolved an oral tradition of passing on important information. Myths and parables were accessible to everybody. Handed down through the ages, passed on from generation to generation they cut across cultural, ethnic and historical boundaries. Myths, as guideposts, have always been there for us and are still in evidence today.

From the earliest of cave drawings to modern books and film, the myths of man have been the creators of man, providing both meaning and symbolism to his and her life. Myths have guided us throughout the centuries and are to be found in every culture. They inspire. They guide. They teach. They provide sustenance and direction as we travel this earthly plane. Since the dawn of time, man has been guided by mythology, and yet, inspired its very nature and course of action. Myths exist for man, while man creates the myths that are lived by. An interesting cycle—one perpetrating the other, as it were.

We don't often think of mythology in our modern age, only as a curiosity, perhaps, but never as a true guide for our journey through life. We refer to other models in this so called advanced age of ours. Yet, we are no different than those of any other age, borrowing our most cherished guideposts from the technological advances of the time. Whatever technology has to offer becomes the model for our functioning, and also the functioning of the world around us, including the larger Universe. Today, it is computer technology and its associated language that provides the framework. Not so long ago, it was the clock and the mathematical formulas that allowed us to split and measure time.

Now we refer to cyberspace and virtual reality as if these define the ultimate in all possible achievement. In the not too distant future, this technology will be viewed as primitive. Not unlike how we view the technology of old black and white television sets with their hand controls and bulbous appearance. Remember, this technology was the epitome of its time in the 1950s. Just like that period, today's technological advances will be rapidly eclipsed in by a new generation of technologies and their adherents, who will speak a language that few of us will understand. The medium of the message may change, as will the message itself perhaps, but their general themes persist.

This is how it goes, what we've come to call progress. One discovery supersedes the last one, and so on. Yet, no technology has ever, and I do mean ever, solved problems associated with our spiritual nature. No advance, no discovery, no matter how far reaching, has ever fulfilled our pursuit of happiness as sustained by our spiritual nature. Happiness is not a function of technological advances; it is a function of the heart. No technology can supersede that.

Where does that leave us? Should we abandon our pursuit of technological advances? Shall we give up improving upon today's computer chip, or whatever successor to that throne is now rising in the wings? Of course not! If technology is not the answer, then what is? Where do we turn for spiritual sustenance?

Do we go back to the Dark Ages where magic, witchcraft and torture were being practiced? Do we dust off the Bible once again and have another go at a proper interpretation? Do we look to the skies for an advancing alien culture that many predict is on the way? Or do we look elsewhere, in a totally different direction, one that the current New Age movement has been pointing to? Where do we look for answers?

Systems of government, as good as they are, are not well functioning entities by any means. Our religious institutions aren't faring any better. Our civic governments are up in arms over one issue or another. Our private industries are in a constant state of flux trying to find the next best solution to meet the bottom line of "more." In recent years, we have seen considerable illegal activity within our financial institutions brought to light, all for the simple aim of making more profit.

Upsizing, downsizing, restructuring are all buzzwords describing the last couple of decades. Where are they taking us? Nowhere near our heart, I would say. In those terms we will be no further ahead than when those cycles began. When there's no guiding spirit or inner direction to call upon, to trust, to guide us forward, where do we turn?

Many of us are anxious right now. In the West we've had the unthinkable—9/11—which has heightened our collective fear. People are wondering what's going to happen next. Few can count on their jobs. There's always a war on somewhere in the world. Families disintegrate. Mad men rule some countries. So-called sane societies continue arming themselves in preparation for the next threat that their defense industries want them to believe is just around the corner.

For what purpose? What is the point? To prove that "might makes right"? That's not going to work. In an ever shrinking world due to globalization, the entire planet has become one neighborhood. Like all good neighbors, we have a mutual investment in the viability and vitality of the community. We reap what we sow; if we sow destruction, we shall receive it in turn. The chemical and radiological misadventures of the past are already oozing out of the Earth, polluting the water and atmosphere and threatening the delicate balance of life. Weaponry and its associated contaminants continue to be developed with full knowledge of the destructive consequences for this planet and its inhabitants.

Yes, there is plenty to be alarmed about. What we have to fear is ourselves and our propensity to destroy that which sustains life. At what point do profit and control cease trumping sanity?

This is what happens when we rely solely upon power, greed and conquest with no accounting for the consequences. When we lie to each other about the hazards we are creating and burying, we are lying to ourselves. And when we lie to ourselves about the wars we engage in, we are on a path of self-destruction, individually and collectively. Myths have already pointed out the folly of such ventures. No authentic myth would ever allow such self-deception. A myth is a living, breathing entity that commands respect by its simple adherence to truth, a truth such as all life forms exist in relation to each other. A truth such as "a lie is a lie" no matter how sophisticated or well spun it is. A truth such as "we reap what we sow" teaches that it is our responsibility to know and respect the consequences of our behavior.

We do not need more false promises. We do need truth. That my friends, is the rub! For if we are to seek the truth then we are in for a big shakeup, a meltdown of thoughts and ideas beyond proportions for which we are ill prepared to recognize. Such is the power of truth and the failing of lies. Ask any addict who's made it to Alcoholics Anonymous. Lies are acceptable only in a world of fantasy and self-denial. Truth is eternally accessible and real. A myth based on truth is available if we reach for it; and only this truth is capable of leading us out of our labyrinth of lies.

"So what," you might say? Who needs such a hard-nosed truth? "I have my home, my car and computer; I have a spouse, children and pets. Why do I need mythology?" Myths help bring context and meaning to our lives beyond which technology and the status quo can provide. Physical life is finite. Between the parameters of birth and death, we want our lives to have meaning.

We call this book mythological because it reaches into the essence of stories told across the years and brings out their truth, a tiny essence that repeats itself over and over in the lives of millions of people across many nations, faiths and cultures. We can couch myths in many forms, but we cannot escape their inherent sincerity and integrity, and their ability to stimulate and to move us toward growth. Myths exist because people create them and people create them because they live their themes. They are also divinely inspired, imbued with a Spirit that transcends culture and time.

Today's myths, if we unearth them, carry the same themes as those of centuries ago. Today's myths are clouded by the media spam that surrounds us, and therefore, are harder to find. They still exist however, as they fill the airwaves of our modern culture and spread their message in every communications medium we have today. We tend not to think in mythological terms anymore. Myths come via today's storytellers. They are couched behind our love of reason and intellect, and are not so close to the heart as they once were. We still live them and imbue our succeeding generations with what we think they mean. We've lost the ability to communicate their themes as effectively as we once did. We're missing many of their vital components, like their ability to touch the Heart and the Spirit which resides within each and every one of us.

We are about to discover our holy purpose on this plane. We need our myths to guide us. Without them, we are in for a very rude awakening. A wake-up call we are unprepared for because of the distance we've traveled away from our center of feeling activity. As the Infinite and Eternal Spirit calls us back, we will most certainly be surprised. How will we handle this? What will we say? We've trekked far and wide on this earthly adventure. The Creator will be expecting a progress report. If we don't expect to connect with the Eternal, what then awaits us?

After knocking on the Creator's door, while not expecting to be invited in, what will we do when that door swings open? Quite a paradox, don't you think? How will we explain this to ourselves, confronted as we will be, by the One who sent us forth on this earthly journey? It is best to dust off those old myths and parables to uncover and resurrect their meaning. Best to return to the root of "all" before our purpose here became convoluted, before we became enraptured by our personality and ego myths which are based in culture and not in Spirit. Spirit is indomitable. Cultural trends come and go. Take a look at the last three decades and see for yourself; music, fashion and pop psychology immediately come to mind.

So where are we going with this? Right into the heart of the matter, to that place where pop culture took precedence and myths fell by the wayside! Right to that place where we all took a wrong turn and followed the wrong god, a god of greed and material accumulation, rather than the God of Spirit. This is where we need to return. Not outside of ourselves as we've come to believe, but inside ourselves where we co-exist in unity with the Great Creator. It is time to wake up and remember!

There is a big adjustment coming in terms of our human and spiritual evolution. Mythology will once again play a vital role in the process. When our usual systems of information processing fail, our tendency as a species is to return to a source of truth and authenticity that has stood the test of time, a familiar old friend we know as myth.

This excursion into myth leads us to where we stand right now; at the doorstep of this new era, the dawn of another epoch, the launching point of this new millennium. At present, we can only speculate at what is coming next and how fast it is moving toward us. Change, transition and transformation are endless cycles. They beat their way to our doorstep and march through our lives. They are as inevitable as the seasons. A major change for all mankind is upon us now.

And what is more important during such turbulent times than faith? Faith, spirituality and self-confidence are tested during such times. If we have only been flirting with the advancing new knowledge and subsequent changes making their way toward us, then we'd better get on board quickly because we're in for the ride of our life, one that we could not anticipate before now. We are on the doorstep of this change, this great leap forward. Why bring up a tired old subject like mythology? That is a very good question. Why should we reach back into the mists of time, of pre-history, for something to propel us forward into this new century and millennium?

Historically, in times of turmoil and chaos, myths were called upon to help explain events, to provide a forum for discussion, to advance the idea that we, the human race, were preparing for the advancing changes. The irony of this is we bring change upon ourselves, and then scramble about to try and make sense of it. We drive change! Long before we formally understood this process, we had myths and parables to describe it. They told us what was coming over the horizon and what we needed to do to get through those inevitable challenges. Myths not only helped us prepare, they helped us execute the changes and adjustments that were essential to the success of the process.

How are we to adapt to this already rapidly moving millennium and the changes that are coming with it? We have to reach into our Souls now for the sustenance we need. There, hidden inside, behind all those roles, addictions and fears we project onto the world, is the energy, the vitality, and the inspiration that will lead us through our great leap forward. Inside all of us is the heart that rings the bell that awakens us to our true destiny. It is no accident that we are here now, at this time in our history. And it is no accident that a great variety of warning bells are sounding. It is up to each and every one of us to access our individual myths and activate them for the times we are in. The threshold of change stands before us. It falls to each of us to consciously step through and assume our responsibility on this journey.

We return to where that Voice pulses within and gives each of us our unique direction. Think of it, seven billion souls whose hearts are beating together, for one simple purpose, to honor the Creator who sent us out and to honor ourselves in this process of on-going evolution. That is the heart of myth and its true purpose. It always points toward the guiding light, the one true beacon that animates all Life. How can you go wrong when you have that light pulsing within?

This is an emotional time. The heartbeat of mythology picks up a bold refrain and leads us onward to our respective destinies, which were charted by the Creator and endorsed by us. Let's look into that world and see where mythmaking can take us.

Feeling Welcome

So how do we know when to stop with our pain and suffering? Is it when we are warmly greeted by a group of like-minded peers? I think so. That's when we know we are no longer alone. Others have suffered just as we are, and made their way to another shore, a place of safety and understanding.

It is true that in our culture we are often made privy to this phenomenon. The plethora of self-help groups testifies to that. For every affliction there is a place to surrender and feel welcome. We no longer have to travel life's path alone.

The Great Creator saw to this from the beginning; "These creatures will have need of each other", and continued to fashion the many legions that would become "Us." We are here to learn from each other and to support each other in the process. Our various circumstances and plights are the challenges we will confront. The manner in which we comfort each other is essential to our success.

There is no harm worse than self-rejection. This is the ultimate in capitulation to those war wounds within. They are there to teach, friend, not to bury you. That would be absurd. Let yourself rejoice whenever you uncover one and bring it to the surface to be shared with warm loving friends. You know who they are, just as you know how to find rejection when you choose to feel worse. We can easily reinforce whatever it is we want to hold on to.

So let your Self be. Let your Self rejoice in the wonderful and amazing world that surrounds you. Let your Self find those friends that have meaningful contributions to make to your existence, as you do to theirs. We are all in this together, aren't we? Let's come out from the dark. Perhaps, you are more than you bargained for. Care to find out?

Introduction from *The Voice*

Greetings friends and neighbors. I am All-That-Is. I come to you through this vehicle named Maurice who is a messenger regarding the dawning of this New Age.

He is here to serve you, as am I. We have been working together for some time now and he is about to launch a number of services where you can gain advice on your personal evolution.

We call this book "Conscious Evolution – Mythology In Action." We also refer to it as mythology's guide because it presupposes some acquaintanceship with mythology, which is your oldest teaching tool on the Earth plane. Maurice has been a fan of mythology since first being re-introduced to it back in the early 80s, your time. I am stepping in at this juncture to help him bring forward all necessary instructional materials at this critical point in time.

Teaching stories have been your best instrument for bringing forth news of an unconventional nature. Guideposts are written into these stories to help address the critical turning points in your lives. Whenever you meet them, mythology provides the necessary references to help you work through the inherent lessons being presented.

At this juncture, the word "Ascension" has made its way into your vocabulary. It signifies something important is about to happen. That being the case, we of the "angelic realms" are here to help you negotiate this path opening in front of you.

So, what is Ascension?

Ascension is the process of reaching for a higher dimension of consciousness rooted in a different set of operating principles than those you are currently accustomed to. The next level on your consciousness scale is the 5th dimension. We are moving you toward this dimension because it takes you where you need to be for the next 1,000 years of earth time.

For those of you unaccustomed to these terms we offer the following. The 3rd dimension of consciousness is where mankind has been for the past few thousand years, since the fall of Atlantis. This is the realm of duality, light and dark, up and down, joy and suffering, us versus them. The 5th dimension of consciousness is unity consciousness, where humans are re-connected with Source, informed by the Heart and aware of their oneness attribute with each other even though appearing as individualized parts of creation. Duality is gone. The feeling of separation no longer exists. There is no us versus them. There is only Oneness and the serenity and joy that accompany that awareness. This is where mankind was before the fall of Atlantis. In your Bible this time is referred to as The Fall which was a fall in consciousness from 5th dimension to the 3rd dimension.

"Why are we not headed for the 4th dimension since we are currently anchored in 3rd dimension density consciousness?"

The 4th dimension of consciousness is simply a passage from the 3rd to the 5th. The 4th dimension is all about healing and recovery from damage accrued through 3rd dimensional life.

Many of you are well along in your recovery and healing process and are at the doorstep of 5th dimension consciousness. This is where the new light and higher dimensional energies are about to be anchored. Fourth dimensional consciousness is like adolescence, a stage that prepares growing individuals for a new way of being. For adolescents, it is moving from childhood into adulthood, a shift that is quite tumultuous as most of you parents well know.

Moving from 3rd dimensional density consciousness to 5th dimensional enlightened awareness is very similar in terms of tumultuous change. Both shifts require a clearing away of the old to prepare for the new. Along with the chaos of any shift comes moments of regression. This is a time of grieving the hopes of returning to simpler times. Eventually, the transition is negotiated and you settle into the new level of being.

Some of you are at the 5th dimension already, but most of you are working your way through the tumult and chaos of the 4th dimensional transition. Maurice has referred to you as "the healing generation," fully engaged in clearing away the family dysfunctions that have held you back to this point. This would include religious dysfunction as well, a topic he will deal with in more detail later on. The bottom line is you are all on your way home to Me! That is, the Me that resides in you!

This process of Ascension is a return to Me, your Creator, your point of origin—Source. This is the end of the line for the ego and all of its petty grievances. This is the end of Earth-Centeredness or 3rd dimensional density consciousness and the beginning of Heart-Centeredness and 5th dimensional reality. Your Heart will be your guide hence forth. Say goodbye to your egos. They have served you well, but are simply not capable of progressing from here.

Your Heart and Soul will be at the helm as you step into this 5th dimension of awareness and light activity. Maurice is making this transition just as you are about to. He too has suffered as many of you are currently. But he is finding his way. How? By keeping his focus on the prize—Ascension and God Consciousness while in a body and living on the Earth.

That is your goal as well and why you are reading this book. Maurice will offer you direction in the coming years as he opens further to his chosen mission. He selected this particular course of action to imbue himself with the details of Ascension, from cleansing the Heart in all its hard-earned glory, to receiving Spirit in gratitude and grace. He wishes to be a fine example of this ascension process in action. He, as each of you, deserves all the rewards that come as a product of ascension into 5th dimension of consciousness.

This author will be delivering messages through the internet and more stories on moving past the heartache that is a feature of 3rd dimensional life. Drawing upon centuries of mythical images and heroic references he will be providing a steady stream of materials designed to help you ascend from every possible angle. His companion book "The Voice – A Mythological Guide to Mankind's Ascension" is one such story you can draw sustenance from as you engage in your own process of emancipation from the 3rd dimension.

Conscious Evolution is about choosing ascension. You must choose ascension as your purpose and goal. It simply will not happen without your willing participation and commitment. Once chosen, it is a gift to be celebrated and pledge allegiance to. Take it into your heart and unwrap it for yourself. No one can do this for you. Please understand, there are no shortcuts through this period of growth and healing. Your emancipation from 3rd dimensional consciousness has to be pursued like any lover you have the strongest desire for. There will be no passive movement into the next realm of conscious awareness. You either choose to go or, by default, you choose to remain behind.

We in the Angelic realms are moving at an accelerated pace now. We have chosen mythology as the favored teaching tool for these times. All the compromises and adjustments that had to be made by your ancestors over the centuries are recorded here. All the accelerations of the Pulse, the drama of change and the blessings gifted by the Gods over millennia have been recorded in your mythology. It is your story of evolution over and over again.

We submit to you that this process of Ascension has been well documented over thousands of years. You need not look elsewhere for true guidance and support. It is all within the framework of mythology and its many tales of heroes and heroines overcoming apparently insurmountable odds. No such thing! You can and have overcome every challenge put in front of you. Now is the time for your graduation.

Digest this book in every manner available to you. Read it and contemplate it, over and over, until you get it. Then open that door to your heart center and let Me come through for you. I am your Creative Source. I am your Point of Origin. I am behind all of your creative abilities and talents. Know that I am You! When we are together there is no master and subject. There is only Us. And, We are One.

Like you, I love to laugh. It is the heartiest of feelings. Notice that word—"heartiest"! Good! Let's get on with it, shall we. Ascension is at your door. Please open it and let Me, Your God Self, come through for you. Let Me embrace you as you so want to embrace Me. Let that be our joy for the next 1,000 years.

The Voice

Evolving

Some messages are cryptic and some are not. But all are issued from the one same source, God the Creator.

When we are alone, contemplating our navel, we risk succumbing to outside interferences. In the ethereal realms there are entities that worry about us because what we do, or not do, affects their future as well. You see, they already know that all the creatures of the Universe are interrelated. What happens to one group affects all the others.

Forget for a moment that they are disappointed with us for proceeding so slowly. Are not the sense of Self and right to be worth pursuing on their own merits? We don't need a cosmic or personal calamity to be reminded of this. For our own sakes, let's evolve. Let's find that place inside where we are centered. Let's find that core of our being and express it gloriously.

Who knows when these entities from other worlds might show up? Don't we want to welcome them with our very best—all aglow and filled with love—so that they can feel at home here too?

We don't have to proceed at anyone's pace but our own. But let's get cracking, shall we. After all, the things we yearn for such as peace and love are contained in that part of us called "Self." It's the Self that actualizes this cosmic love in our world where physical bodies roam. Our Soul is there to guide us, but our Self does the actual work. And when we graduate, we and our Soul are larger for the exercise.

Let's get on with our tasks, shall we. After all, the God of Love created us and is waiting for our return Home.

1 – The Hero Myth

"This above all: to thine own self be true,
And it must follow, as the night the day,
Thou canst not then be false to any man."
William Shakespeare – *Hamlet*

When we think of life, we think of many things. We think of the life force coursing through our veins. We think of life everlasting as charted for us in religious texts. Without life, our world is devoid of meaning. The absence of life is nothing, not death, but nothing. Can we actually conceive of nothing? Of course not! Not even death. Because with death, its contemplation has to occur from the context of life.

There simply is no absence of life. We acknowledge that to contemplate life from the point of view of life is a tautological argument. We have to be alive to contemplate its presence and absence. In mythology, all struggles are about life and death. Heroes and heroines conquer one polarity in order to fully grasp the other. They face death, or rather, their fear of death, in order to become filled with life.

This is the eternal cycle—life, death and rebirth. All heroes learn this and accept this. It is part of their struggle and their destiny. They must overcome fear to gain this truth. Fear is the enemy of life. It is fear that needs to be embraced. Life without death is not life and life without consciousness is mere existence.

Death does not exist except as a counterpoint to life. Death gives life its meaning by framing it within a limited context. This death we speak of is not a real death; it is merely an absence of incarnate life. Life without death is illogical; but death, in and of itself, is simply an abstraction. Nothing dies; it only transforms. The first law of thermodynamics states that no matter can be created or destroyed, it can only be transformed. All heroic journeys are journeys of transformation: from one form to another, from one dimension to another, until graduation occurs again, and we move on to another form.

In ancient times these transformations were charted in myths. Myths described and explained the needed energies, flights of fancy, whimsical adventures and demons to confront. Myths provided guidance to a population hungry for answers, in need of charts and graphs, glyphs perhaps, to move them along. A living, breathing mythology became legendary, leading scores of men and women through the trials and tribulations of life's important transitions. Recall that most myths are about transformation in particular, and transformation is the sine qua non of all myths. This was especially true for those tales that described the hero's welcome return from confronting death in the underworld to his or her regaining a more conscious life on the earth plane.

The Hero Myth is the most favored of them all, and the one we see replayed today in many action-adventure films. Heroes and heroines lead the way into the New Age. They are the groundbreakers of our future. We are on such a threshold again, preparing to leap toward a new cosmic unity, ready to break new ground and chart a new course. How can we apply classic mythology in today's world and toward what end?

Jesus Christ, the Buddha and Mohammed, among others, implored us to listen to our hearts. Plato and many fellow Greek philosophers advised, "Know Thyself." Shakespeare wrote in Hamlet: "To thine own self be true." Over the years of our recorded history, many teachers, prophets and mentors repeated the same advice. This very guidance comes to us again through modern day psychologists, medical practitioners, artists and spiritual advisors.

Before the above proponents had their say, mythology was delivering that very advisement. In fact, many modern day proponents of "getting to know your Self" refer back to certain myths to underline their point. Freud did it. So did Carl Jung, along with numerous others over the last century. Myths are still guideposts to the modern era. They're not so visible anymore. They've suffered from the bad press of being synonymous with fiction.

Joseph Campbell, an anthropological researcher from the latter part of the 20th century, demonstrated how myths and parables crossed cultural boundaries and were recycled through succeeding generations. He pointed out, for example, how the Hero Myth appeared in all ancient cultures and has survived through untold generations to be recycled again and again. We find these myths today in movies, television, books and musical lyrics. We still rely on the Hero Myth, and one of my favorite examples is "The Deer Hunter." The main character, Michael, goes through every aspect of Joseph Campbell's heroic triad. It consists of Separation, Initiation and Return which are well documented in this brilliant story; separation of himself from familiar referents, initiation through trial and tribulation in the context of war, and return to his familiar world with greater awareness and appreciation of himself and the people that surround him.

There are also comparisons to modern psychology. Carl Jung spoke of the "collective-unconscious" which, in mythical lore, was related to Psyche, a goddess, whose function it was to inform humans on their condition and plight, and advise on possible solutions. She, too, was instrumental in imploring heroes and heroines to know themselves. Modern psychology is, in part, derived from this source and owes its very name to that mythical goddess, Psyche, from antiquity.

Psychology, which is my field, is about getting to know yourself, using the tools of the trade—testing, psychotherapy, counseling, clinical investigations, and so on. Pop psychology is about getting to know yourself for $15.95 over a weekend. Getting to know ourselves isn't going to happen that easily or economically. My own experience, both personal and professional, is that the process is long term, with every step of the journey having its own challenges and rewards. A good book can help, but is only one chapter in the entire process of getting to know ourselves.

What we are witnessing today, as the new millennium unfolds, is transformation and getting to know ourselves on a grand scale. Already, we are being told about this. Economic structures, social structures, religious structures and, therefore, personal structures are changing dramatically. Like it or not, the process is upon us. The New Age sections of bookstores are full of such references, and these also cross over into pop psychology, parapsychology, philosophy and religion. Just check out your favorite bookstore. Looking through these sections in today's bookstores begs the question: "Why is there such a plethora of mythically based reference material being delivered to us right now?" To announce the advance of the New Era is the answer! It is already here and our choice is whether or not we deal with it.

Our current structures for understanding life do not account for this New Age information. We need different reference points to guide us through this transitional period. We need guideposts that override the limits of modern terminology and that can trace their roots back through the mists of time so they can be consistently relied upon. Such guideposts are like the needle in a magnetic compass, always pointing in the same direction—towards the Self, the true north and center of our spiritual and feeling nature.

It is this mantra, "To thine own self be true," we repeat over and over again. Right here, right now. That is the sine qua non of our era. We cannot move forward as individuals and as a species without this most important central resource. Our Self is our guide to our creativity, our life purpose and the Creator. And this true and authentic Self will take us to the core of our being, our Soul! That is where we are headed. That is what defines the current challenge.

When myths are alive they breathe spiritual energy into the population. They help all listen and understand that their true purpose in life is much larger than what they've witnessed thus far. Behind the scenes of our common everyday life, there is another play unfolding. One that will see each of us reaching the greatest of heights, which in our regular circumstances, we would have not thought possible.

From the perspective of myth, such achievements are always possible. Within that context, we can and do supersede our highest aspirations. We confidently go where we never thought we would. And we go deeper within than we could ever have conceived. As Christ said, "greater things than these shall ye do." There are no limits. There are only greater levels of conscious awareness, personal satisfaction, emotional growth and heart-guided achievement.

We are at an important threshold, a crossroads of purposes. We can live out our life in our everyday circumstances or we can transcend these and go further than we ever thought possible. The Hero Myth can lead the way. This has to be a myth grounded in spiritual truth, imbued with divine fire, and sustained by love. Only such a living, breathing myth can lead us forward. Let us see what this vehicle of myth looks like!

Opening Your Heart

What is it with this open-heart business? Isn't this a tough requirement for us humans? Oh yes, we can easily say: "open your heart and you will receive the best life has to offer." But doesn't this include pain too? Well, yes it does. We all know this one, don't we? So why ascribe such importance to this open-heart concept? Isn't that a prescription for danger?

"Not at all. I never meant to harm you with this open-heart idea, only to alert you that Earth school requires it if you're going to be successful."

"I sent you here on a mission, to learn all that you can, and to notice that those of you with open hearts enjoyed the greatest success with life's experiences. Yes, they did feel pain along with their joy and other satisfactions. They felt life completely. That is My measure of success."

"For those of you who block your pain, you are at a disadvantage. Those things you block and fail to feel are there anyway, only locked up in some vault that you created within yourself. They appear lost, but actually remain present like an untreated infection, which won't go away until you squeeze out the hurt."

"That's when a heart is truly open, after it is healed from every blow thrown in its direction. Life becomes safer then because you've developed tolerance. And tolerance breeds openness, as I've described to you before."

"So take a good look at yourself before you close that vault door. Make sure that all your hurts are out. Then you'll be able to proceed fully charged and ready for the challenges ahead. That's why you need an Open Heart. And that's where you can access Me in the bargain."

2 – A Hero's Welcome

"Once upon a time," we say when a new story crosses our lips. We pull them out of an apparent void and share them with each other as a way of communicating understanding on important information. We convey much to each other through storytelling and the medium of myth. We teach each other about love, honesty, depravity, cold-heartedness, sensitivity, levity, humor, lust, ambition, level-headedness, sensibility, humility, all of the great human attributes, and all their lowly counterparts.

We pass on these lessons because we believe it is right and necessary. We want the next generation to benefit from what we have learned. They, in turn, will pass on these lessons and what they are learning for themselves. The succession of knowledge passed from one hand to the next, across millennia, across cultures, has been essential to succeeding generations.

Sadly, we turned away from myth, so enamored have we become with the latest technology. In the pursuit of quick fixes, we lost our connection to the human spirit. We lost sight of death. We lost sight of life. As mentioned earlier, we know we cannot understand one without an appreciation of the other. Without the lessons of myth we are topsy-turvy, turned upside down and without a rudder. Simply put, we are lost and scrambling to find our way out of the chaos.

Chaos typically breeds feelings of fear, confusion, impotence and uncertainty. Drugs, alcohol, gambling, and so many other addictive substances and practices are the road well-traveled by many who are seeking some type of relief. Love and hate play themselves out regularly in this theatre of addiction and denial. Love and hate are the classic themes of myth and poetry. Love and hate become entangled in this arena, because the addictive processes we turn to are poor substitutes for what we really need, and that is an informed life. Addiction reflects a sense loss, ineptitude, dissatisfaction and fear, experiences we don't want to deal with. In the presence of these, many individuals choose to numb themselves. Numbing appears as a method of coping when spirit is not available.

This response to chaos contributes to further chaos. An informed life is filled with spirit, meaning and direction. This is where a healing journey can begin. All healing journeys lead back to spirit or "home," our true core and feeling nature, our connection with the Divine.

All healing journeys are quests. They represent the quest of the hero, one that is played out in a new format, a new millennium format which we will call the "path of recovery." This is it in our modern times. The hero's journey is a healing journey, and millions of people are traveling this path worldwide. They are twelve-stepping, educating themselves in seminars, looking for truer ground through therapy and group work, seeking their inner Self while venturing forth into the darkness of their existence. This is a true heroic journey. This is mythology in action for today's culture.

This is the path of the wounded man and the wounded woman, the traumatized child and the confused adolescent. There are innumerable variations of this tale, and they are all truly heroic. There is no doubt of that. Ask someone who is on the path, one who has traveled some distance on their healing journey and has disabled some of their formidable demons. Yes, the path charted by the hero myth is clearly evident today.

Wherever people gather is where one can confront oneself. Not so long ago people met at oases and watering holes. Camel drivers and silk traders came together to exchange goods and ideas. People meet today in churches, bazaars, universities and theatres continuing the practice of exchanging ideas and services. Yesterday's bazaars have become today's shopping malls.

Shopping malls are filled with people looking for something. Some are engaged in a process of numbing while others are searching for something that will make them bolder, braver and stronger. The same adventurers who are seeking their true Selves are crossing paths with people who are avoiding life while gorging themselves with food or clothes or some other distraction, hoping for a miracle to fill their empty hearts. Hearts that could be filled with spirit instead of being filled with the goods and services of 1001 merchants eager to please an aching population.

Interesting places are these shopping malls. What does this have to do with heroes and heroines? All persons are mirrors to each other, and malls offer the largest, most multifaceted mirrors of all. They are today's watering holes, town plazas, and bazaars. They offer glimpses into many possible realities, from the poorest to the richest, from the gross to the sublime, with multiple variations in between.

For now we will limit ourselves to this mirroring aspect. This is where heroic journeys begin. Somewhere, somehow, something has to strike you and reflect something back to you about your life. That jolt of recognition will take place in the mirroring eyes of another. All eyes are mirrors to the Soul.

Others may be looking at you for the same reason, to see what they can learn about themselves. There is reciprocity, a give and take, which is the nature of all life. There is no giving without receiving. All cycles have their counterpoints which keep them in balance. As soon as you know this, you've gleaned an important awareness. This important and fundamental fact, that the Earth is an ever expanding, ever evolving series of cycles, points and counterpoints, is played out in the macrocosm and microcosm of your life and mine.

Like it or not, we interrelate. We all affect each other in perceptible and imperceptible ways. These are more significant than we realize, because we are each a turn in this eternal web, and our turn sets someone else's turn in motion. That is, we influence each other and we need each other. We need our Self too, in very significant fashion, more so than many of us realize. It is our lost Self we are pursuing. That is our goal as aspiring heroes and heroines. We are on a quest, to our Self, our real Self, our Sacred Self.

Our Self is the true center of our being and the place from which our individual truth emanates. It's where we can come to know our passions, our place in the world, our purpose and our destiny. Without our Self we truly have nothing except the mainstream reference and structures around us which are now crumbling. The evidence is clear; we hear about it daily from the media. Politicians and religious authorities are falling from grace because they have violated a private and public trust. Religion is in decline due to loss of relevance and diminishing attendance. The middle class is crumbling due to outsourcing of jobs and diminished purchasing power. Crumbling does not mean total disintegration, although some would argue that is indeed the case. Rather, it means a serious reshuffling.

The signs and symbols that define this rising era point to the Self as the true center of the personality and the Soul as its spiritual counterpart. Ego, as the personality's central authority, now belongs to the dying era we are leaving behind. Self and Soul are rising in its place and are inextricably intertwined. They are one and the same at a fundamental level, like the way "particle" and "wave" are used interchangeably to describe the electron. Self and Soul are flip sides of the same coin. They come from our Divine Nature which resides within. You, we, I are the source of our being and a home for this Divinity. You, we, I, are God, incarnate.

If I say to you, "Trust your Self, believe in your Self, be your Self", can you in any way go wrong? Can you say, "He's lying or mistaken; I shouldn't, can't, won't trust my Self?" Or would you say, "I can't trust him because he's telling me to trust me?" You can already see that this argument becomes circular and absurd. Trusting your Self and connecting with your Soul are essential to revealing who you are. And from that perspective, they cannot be questioned. If you can't trust your Self and you can't acknowledge your Soul, then where do you stand? Authenticity demands that you be true to your Self. Only an authentic Self can be authentic with others.

Here is the inherent beauty of myths. Whether they are a story or a parable, their simple truth is undeniable and unmistakable because they point to you. They are a mirror to you. You are free to use them or not, to agree with their premise or not. They are not dictates, they are reference points. What does it mean to "Trust Your Self"? From myth's point of view, it means feel what you feel, speak your truth, acknowledge your mistakes, do your very best, pray for guidance and "listen!" Listen to that guidance that emanates from within you, from your heart and feeling center. There it is in action, your feelings, your inner guidance; the "I am that I Am" all at work within you, showing you the truth about you.

Here is an important parameter which is everyone's responsibility, and that is "first, do no harm." This means your awareness and expression of feeling must not bring harm to yourself or others. That would be contrary to your Divine Nature. With that in mind, how can you go wrong? You can't. How can you say no to your Self? Go forward on your path with hope, determination and clear-headedness, and activate that power that is yours. So you can be true to you, which is the Creator in you, and bring forward those gifts which are yours to share with the world.

Every once in a while something happens in life that shakes us up. For some, it could be a course of study. For others, it could be a movie, a life crisis, a particular song, a major loss or trauma. A crisis or major loss can be a call to awaken. One of my own significant challenges began several years ago after my wife was diagnosed with Multiple Sclerosis. I was frightened. I began listening more closely to what was going on within. I had been a fairly traditional psychotherapist, plying my craft as I was trained to do. Mixing intuition with other forms of guidance was part of my style and had served me well to that point. One day, after this crisis hit, I began writing. Actually, I felt compelled to write. I wrote stories, poetry and music with a spiritual bent and mythical flavor. All of this material was growth oriented. All these writings had similar themes in regards to knowing Self, being true to Self, waking up to Soul, including children's spirituality, song lyrics and poetic reflections. From these writings came my first book of Parables, then another, and another, until I had several manuscripts on these subjects. Mythology, spirituality and personal growth were now moving through me, thanks in part to that particular life crisis. This had been my wake-up call.

What is trying to be born through you, my friend? What are your gifts and passions telling you? Expressing creativity is our challenge. We all have this capability. We are built to handle this challenge. Our inherent design, as spiritual and physical beings, naturally drives us toward creativity and innovation. Watch children. They create without inhibition. It is their nature. It is ours too!

Self & Ego

"Once upon a time there was a sad man who threw away his life to have more control over his world." Doesn't make a lot of sense, does it? Throwing away your life to have more control! Shows you what can be done with an odd set of operating values.

We take ourselves out into the world to learn lessons. Sometimes we are poorly informed and come back from our ventures more messed up than when we left. It's this kind of application, based on false premises, that leads us astray, down the garden path to our own destruction.

Ever wonder why there are so many "burnouts" today? Same reasoning as above. Apply your voluminous intellect to a situation requiring emotional intelligence and then watch out for that wall! Here it comes again, straight at you.

The Self knows better than this. And when ego is set aside, the Self can do wondrous things. This central aspect will lead you right back on to your proper path and have you call upon your emotional intelligence along the way. Know that challenges on this road are there to wake you up from that docile sleep imposed on you by ego and forces around you.

The Universe has marvelous ways of reminding us to make a course correction when we've strayed onto another's prescribed path rather than sticking to our own. Bouncing off walls and hitting dead ends come to mind. There are numerous others. You could name a few if you thought about it. Just know that you can rise to this challenge and get back on your own path?

Give it a try. Look out for yourself. Learn to identify what is uniquely your own. Choose for yourself, based on your emerging values and creative desires. Yes, there are dangers out there and walls can be counted among them. But maybe there's a path around that wall? If you don't see one, make your own. Discover what you are made of. It will be worth it.

3 – Heroes and Heroines

Heroes and heroines of all types have come to pass on this Earth following in the footsteps of other seekers. So many have faded into the mists of time it becomes impossible to count them all. What we can surmise is that, in all of these comings and goings, a repository of mythical images has been left behind. And those, like me, who are here to explore and record these artifacts, have begun to pick through the pieces, fashion them together and return them to a population hungry for spiritual sustenance.

Not so long ago these mythical guideposts were handed down to new generations through an oral tradition designed to pass on the traditional ways. That system doesn't work anymore because the current media storm has bombarded us with convoluted and contradictory messages about our place in the world. A spiritually hungry population needs something solid to feed on, something with substance that includes all those dynamics of the human condition, something beyond which today's media has to offer. In the theatre of life there is comedy, drama, pathos, conflict and resolution.

We study bards, prophets, philosophers and theologians to get a glimpse of their Souls, in order to have a glimpse of our own. I'm not sure why we do this anymore. I decided to visit, but vowed I would never rest in those realms for fear of confounding myself. Their reflections have been recycled and distorted so many times over the years they have lost much of their original meaning and value. In my opinion, today's Christianity does not represent Christ's teachings. The fact that church pews are emptier than ever is clear testimony that this religious approach has lost touch with the heart.

At the beginning of my search, I revisited the Christianity of my childhood and found, once again, that it could not fill my cup. I still hoped that Jesus, the man, would be relevant for me today. But now I know that he cannot. Religion's interpretation of his message has been so distorted that it has lost its relevance to me and to the world in which I live. I hope his original message surfaces again, as a Christ consciousness through me, through you, through all of us. In my view, the church and its misrepresentation of the historical Jesus has nothing left to teach. Scripture is consistently being used for some political or social agenda and the church is clearly party to this.

The disenfranchisement of women, blacks, homosexuals and divorced persons continues to prevail. Such groups have been either left behind or simply condemned as sinners. Challenging the traditional church and its interpretations of Christ's teaching has been labeled as heresy. By so doing, religious authorities have bound us to the past and thwarted our pursuit of authentic spiritual growth. These were not the teachings of Christ. His original contributions to mythology have yet to be fully retrieved.

We must take responsibility for ourselves now. We cannot solely count on a historical figure to rescue us. If we allowed this, we would deny our free will and the opportunity to do it for ourselves. Our time at the helm of our lives has just begun. We have a long journey ahead of us. Jesus, mythical giant that he was, has pointed the way. But we have to make the heroic descent into the unconscious realms of our lives to pursue certain necessary confrontations such as our fears, our hurts and our traumas. Jesus spent 40 days in the desert challenging his beliefs. Ultimately, he was resurrected. It is now time to face our personal challenges and secure our own resurrection.

Many questions are posed when we come to a point like this in our story. Where does it all begin? What is the first step? How do I do this? I've asked all of these questions and wondered about what I needed to do. But inevitably, I had to take charge. This is not a new message. Hearing it repeatedly can become tiresome. But taking charge remains a necessity. Initially I was craving solace and hoping for a reprieve from my responsibilities. It eventually came, but not in a form I expected. It never came from without; it came from within. I know you've heard this before. Our reprieve is not coming from anywhere but within.

I have used my own life experiences as examples of how Self and Soul can erupt into your life. I have lived what I am writing and sharing what I've learned here. All through my years of therapeutic practice I saw this type of inspiration, with Self and Soul behind the scenes, surface for many individuals.

When unhealthy defensive strategies are removed from positions of guarding the personality, the creative river flows. This can be startling in the beginning. When we're accustomed to protecting ourselves from real or imagined dangers, allowing our inner Self to be expressed can be quite challenging. Most people would believe that opening oneself up should be easy. Not so! A well-defended, closed person can be taken aback by this new found creativity. However, knowing that this change is coming about can easily temper this tumultuous creative thrust.

So what does all this mean for you? If you've been feeling that urge to write, paint, build, construct or sing then be aware that your creativity is calling to you. This creativity comes to you through your Self, from your Soul. The phrase "to be called" is found regularly in mythology. Various prophets and many modern writers, such as Hermann Hess and Thomas Merton, have used such terms to describe their creative awakening. This process can be intimidating. It is the power of that call that makes it so. If you're feeling something powerful stirring inside, then it is time for you to listen.

Remember this invitation to listen. Listening to ourselves is not so easy when we're accustomed to battling our inner critic. That part of us will keep repeating that "we're not good enough," "we'll never achieve our goals," or "we are not worthy". This is the voice of doom, not of reason.

It's the sound of our own discouragement echoing through us. To solve this may require some detective work. Did you do this to yourself? Or, were these negative messages imposed on you by external sources such as teachers, parents and other authority figures?

The truth is many of us did receive a good dose of this negativity which continues to weigh heavily upon us. The voice coming from your Self and Soul, that voice that resides within, is urging you to try new things, express yourself and take a chance on yourself. That voice is calling you now and wants you to listen. How do you feel about that? Frightened? This is often how it feels at the beginning of an awakening process. It is scary because all your protective personality defenses are being challenged. Your defenses want you to remain hidden while your Self wants to become conscious and free.

Your Self, your piece of the Divine, needs to come through you. It will never happen without your consent. All the energy you've put into defending yourself can now be applied to creativity, to actualizing your piece of the cosmic puzzle. If you don't do it, then that piece, your piece, will remain missing from the larger picture. Have you ever tried to finish a jigsaw puzzle with a number of key pieces missing? Frustrating isn't it? I suspect that's how the Creator feels, seeing us scurry under the coffee table looking for the missing piece. The Creator appreciates it may be some time before all parts of the cosmic puzzle are assembled. The Creator is patient, though, and will wait as long as necessary.

That Divine part of us never gives up. Never! It is always there, encouraging, praising, suggesting, and nudging us along. That part of us invariably believes in our capabilities and celebrates when we begin to express our true nature. The Divine becomes excited when we try something new, when we experiment with a different way of being, when we pick up those notebooks, crayons, paints, musical instruments and college calendars. It knows that the dream, that beautiful blue flame of creativity is still alive! The dream, that fantasy we play for ourselves, inside our hearts, when no one is around to discourage or judge us, is calling. This dream features us as heroine or hero, doing what it is we secretly want to do, expressing that passion that rises in us like a tidal wave. At times, we get so excited we could burst. That's your passion, trying to make its way to your awareness. It wants you to recognize it and activate its switch.

We are all on this journey together, learning from each other, sharing and mirroring back and forth the images of our lives. They all count, most especially, most certainly your own! So take hold now and prepare yourself as we journey further into the hinterlands of our existence, as we explore and examine that phenomenon we call life from the point of view of myth. These are the myths that you and I—all of us—are living, that propel us forward on this quest through time, that drive the engine of our Souls in great anticipation of our arrival. To where? To your home, your Self, your Soul and spiritual consciousness, all of these waiting for you at the very center of your being.

Growing

Sometimes it's hard to make a change in our lives. It requires such stamina, a wealth of desire. Is it any wonder many give up before they start? The aching inside drives us forward, to a hopefully better place, where we can be relieved of our dissatisfaction.

So where do we go on this quest? Do we cross the mighty ocean? Scale the tallest mountain? Or simply take stock of ourselves and issue another edict. "I will not live like I did before," "I will change the script of my life," "I will scale what is mine to scale, and I will go it alone if I have to."

There is no need to go it alone. The Great Creator is always there with a helping hand. He is right behind you, giving a little push. Saying things like, "You can do more if you want," "There is much you have to offer," "You're just getting started." A gentle prodding it will be, because She's sensitive that way. Pushing too hard elicits resistance. That's not the way to go. Gentle prodding, with generous doses of encouragement, will take you further.

It can be scary out there. To leave the familiar shore and reach for the unknown, that takes courage. But isn't that what your heart wants, to explore further and move out of the familiar to try something new?

We all have definitions of ourselves: "My aunt said this about me, my dad said that, the teacher agreed," and so on. They provide us with a launching point based on what they can see. But remember, they have limitations too. They see what they can handle. If there's genius in the offing, then they are likely out of their league and someone else will have to step up to help out. More often than not, that's our Self.

That part of us that rises later in life, needs us to take the helm, to risk, if necessary, all that we have in favor of a better, less scripted existence. We all have more to offer than we are aware, certainly more than others may think. They can only see as far as their limitations permit. If we are to deliver all that we have, then we have to serve it up ourselves. By our permission do we rise!

Take that step now. Give yourself permission to rise. Open your heart, see what's inside and push a little. It'll come out on its own then. Once freed, it knows where to go, just like a flower knows how to reach for the sun. It's your turn now. Let it be so.

4 – Life as Movie and Myth

The magic of time is limitless. Each generation brings to the scene a potpourri of resources designed to stir the imagination. Today, it is the movie theatre, a symbol of an advanced society to some, a mystery to others and a joy for most. The screen of our real lives brings to us an abundance of mythical images. On the screen of a theatre these images are played out for us by heroes and heroines of all stripes engaged in the great variety of life's many challenges. The movie screen lights up and offers us the opportunity for another journey into our psyche. We project our life challenges onto the movie screen where we can all take them in. The producers do the work of rehashing the mythical themes of life. We absorb the result and ponder what this may mean for our own lives.

In recent times, movies have become more artful, more subtle, more sophisticated and certainly more advanced. With advances in technology and special effects, they create an illusion, take us to places we've never been and teach us something about ourselves in the process. They allow us to laugh and to cry while offering us experiences that we would not have otherwise. They expose us to a great variety of avenues offered by life. They teach us about relationships to ourselves, to others, and to the world around us. In turn, they teach us to appreciate each other.

Each vignette that lights up the movie screen carries with it a basic and hopeful message. The human spirit is alive and well, and we can see our mythical heritage being played out on the theatre screen. The major themes of life are cast into movies and we can appreciate them from our own perspective. Movies advise us of life's many avenues and innumerable possibilities.

We don't have to live out every challenge in life. We can watch and learn some of those themes vicariously. This way, we are exposed to a multiplicity of events that can affect a person's life and see the more favorable responses played out. In this day and age, we are witness to a multitude of mythical images delivered to us through personal experience and the experiences of others. Pay attention! The smallest of cues may hold an important key to finding your way "home."

Mythical images have purpose. They convey a message and deliver a point. Their many characters and players set the stage for what the seeker is about to learn. We are all main characters at some point in our lives and bit players at other times. This is the scene in which we participate and follow whenever a life lesson unfolds. Lessons, big and small, are played out in larger than life mythical tales such as the stories of Hercules and Ulysses. Other lessons, big or small, can show up in subtler forms such as in the movie *The Heart is a Lonely Hunter*. We get a taste of everything somewhere along the way if we are living consciously.

When a man and a woman meet on the movie screen of life they set in motion the mythical imagery of the centuries gone before them. All that has been learned about emotions and relationships are brought to the fore and played out in this new drama. Such lessons are universal and played out repeatedly beginning with Adam and Eve moving through Romeo and Juliet, and on to today's *When Harry Met Sally*.

We watch; we enjoy; we appreciate. We see ourselves as one of the characters. We see the circumstances as if they are happening to us. We view what transpires with this couple and our feelings about it not realizing an old play is afoot. These protagonists represent millions of players over the years and have been portrayed in many theatrical performances, reminding us of what has been learned about relationships to this point.

When mythical imagery enters the scene, it cuts to the core of the human drama. That is where the heart is and where the stakes are highest. Each man and each woman, playing out their scene, are unaware that a myth is being re-enacted. When acting consciously, they can know that they are part of a larger fabric, a piece of life's web that they are able to construct and then return the lessons learned to the whole of life experience. In so doing, we continue to invest in and refine the myths of yesteryear into the present. Movies contextualize yesterday's myths. This is mythology in action. Myths never die, they only change form.

If mythology is fact based, then each play or movie is one representation of that fact, and one example of a particular genre of myth. For example, the myth of the hero is the most widely known and is found in every culture. Joseph Campbell is one researcher of myth who deciphered and described their main parameters. He clearly demonstrated that all myths are a derivative of one Master Myth, the Hero Myth, with each referring back to the basic structural sequence of "separation, initiation and return." Heroes leave the surface world to go underground and deal with dark mysterious forces. Once there, they go through a psychological cleansing process via the challenges they encounter and the lessons they learn about themselves. They then return to the surface of their lives enlightened, stronger, wiser and share that knowledge with the world.

Heroes and heroines often enter a path of service after having passed through their personal trials. When they are fully healed they have much to offer. Even if they are not, they can still be an example and teach what they have learned. It may not be the entire heroic scenario, but their contributions will still have value.

Heroes and heroines go to the well of transformation many times. Internally, they are brought back to that place where they are still blocked. They move on when they surrender to the forces that guide them and follow their cleansing template. While they are stuck, such as Prometheus' foot in a rock, we see that they are driven and unable to take flight. An uncompleted journey shows someone still struggling, caught by some archetype, unable to move forward until new information is at hand or some old belief is surrendered to the truth now standing before them. A completed journey shows a man or woman at peace with their Selves.

The heroic journey is paradoxical. Life brings us back to that place from which we need to free ourselves. This may be some trauma or psychic rupture from childhood that obstructed our evolutionary path. Many of our mythical stories are symbolic of this state of affairs. Sometimes it's a life in ruin or a state of contradiction from which the hero is trying hard to break free. Some important new player steps in and moves us along. As an example, a depressed young woman steps into a drug store to buy medications with the intent to overdose. An elderly man approaches her and offers a rose which someone had passed on to him. The young woman accepts the rose, leaving the drug store and her intentions of self-harm behind. She enters a nearby hospital, eyes a patient in a hallway and offers the rose. One person with one small gift made a huge difference in another person's life. Our heroine returned to her path and resumed her journey of growth. The rose was timely and broke the spell. While paying her helper's gift forward, she renewed her faith in life and herself. Today, I know her to be vibrantly alive, having moved forward into a life of service.

There are many important characters in all forms of the heroic journey. We never make it on our own. We are guided, nudged, pushed, shoved or propelled into our unique direction. Often, we all need a kick or a gift to get back on track.

We do this for each other all the time, often unwittingly. We inspire, guide and teach each other. We motivate, challenge and support. We are every actor and bit player. We are all of these because we are living and breathing mythology, and we exude this power from our very core. When we see it and feel it, it becomes magic. At that point we know that we are one with the Creator, God, Spirit and Consciousness.

To learn more about yourself read a mythical story or two, preferably one that has themes paralleling your own life. There are only a few versions of the main mythical adventure that are re-worked over and over again so its dominant parameters will soon become visible and familiar. That's when we begin to see ourselves everywhere. We follow ourselves into the next scene. We check out of the action from time to time to review what we've learned, and then return to the fray prepared to learn more.

This is a play that bears repetition. We are venerable creatures capable of much more than we realize. We move into a more extraordinary realm of consciousness, a source of energy and thought in action, playing itself out in a never ending variety of roles and situations. Beggar, thief, prince, pauper, Christian, Muslim, Jew are roles from which we can sample. We try them on through identification with various characters available to us through movies, plays and books. It is school of a sort. We sample as much as we can. We may identify our favorites early in the process, but not commit to them until the taste testing is over. We apply ourselves to a variety of situations, events, characters, crises, love, joy, hate. We trade hats with each other and try on each other's roles. At times we may be living someone else's life vicariously, and they may be living ours. We're not always conscious of this, but some part of us is paying attention, as we may be reminded later.

We try on lots of roles and experiment with various patterns of behavior. After a time, we choose our favorites, those that feel most in sync with who we are. We wear these with greater comfort and regularity. A teacher, by nature, usually teaches. A healer, by nature, usually heals. Within each of these possibilities, a number of additional choices are available. These would be opportunities to specialize and develop a specific talent for personal or professional application. The great mosaic of life reveals many amazing opportunities and achievements. We have a lifetime to polish the jewel of our talents. Practice makes perfect!

We focus on our true nature at this point. We set out to refine our particular talents and abilities. That means repetition from several different perspectives, with less venturing into alien territory. That would defeat our individual purpose. We want to be good at what we're capable of doing, so we specialize. This is the point. The Creator needs specialists in all the important avenues of human experience. People with experience get the job done.

That is where we, aspiring heroes and heroines, enter the stage. We are the ones the Creator is looking for, the ones that are required now. The Creator has called out to this Army of Light, heroes and heroines coming together in this grand mythical adventure to help bring home an awakening humanity.

This is an awesome task. Humanity is poised on the brink of a great leap forward. The Army of Light is coming together to help usher in this new consciousness. No one knows with any certainty how this is coming about, but many of us have felt it coming for a number of years. We've seen this awareness grow and expand within the past years to include an understanding of our place on this planet and our relationship with all its inhabitants. This growing awareness is now visible in such areas as climate change, personal growth, human rights and our interdependence with each other nationally and internationally. This knowledge has been spearheaded and modeled by those of us who have broken through to the new consciousness. We are now aware that only through responsible action can we bring about meaningful change.

Mythical images prepare us for these times as do breakthrough movies like "Avatar." They teach us about many things including love, empathy, courage, perseverance, truth and honesty. They teach us to be open and to seize new ideas and opportunities. They teach us to recognize truth. Right now, the truth needs to be known. Not the truth for all times, but truth for this moment. This is our task. Some would say that we signed up for this prior to incarnating this time around. Others would say that our collective unconscious is beginning to surface. We can only know this in our hearts, where our individual truth lies. No authority figures or institutions can help us here. That is why we rely on mythology as our guide. It has an unmistakable air of truth about it, and because it resonates as being honest, it offers emotional satisfaction at the same time. Mythical imagery is never deceptive. It holds the truth at its core. We need to connect to that core which is the center of our being; this is our heart center and our Soul.

We are not deceived when acting from this core. All heroes and heroines learn this; to trust themselves, their felt version of truth, love, justice and freedom. All mythical images have these qualities and have been relied upon throughout the centuries as a valuable resource.

The Creator, through us, wrote all these myths as guideposts to our journey here on Earth. We can play them out and learn through the directions they provide. We are not without hope when we have these images at our disposal. They are the unvarnished truth. They are ever present and come into our awareness when we are ready to receive them. Like children screaming with delight, without reserve or judgment, they are comprised of unbridled joy, fear, hope, loss and adventure. They are the great emotions and spiritual awakenings of the world. They comprise the core of human experience.

Myths never fail to appease or inspire. They provide comfort and guidance in times of disarray, chaos and uncertainty. That time is here. As we face this new millennium, we look for hope, direction and comfort. We want to feel safe, and myths can provide that with its indelible referents. We are here to learn more about ourselves and each other, and myth can help us map a sound way home.

We need myth to drive us toward our goals, to show us what can be done and to teach us how to do it. We are here for a purpose and that purpose is to learn. We learn about our lives through myth. We learn that the Creator is with us and we can call that energy into our life movie at any moment. The Creator is the inspiration behind myth, and all myths lead back to the Creator, their point of origin and our final destination. Full circle, we return to the beginning, the Source, which is the Creator within each and every one of us.

Asking for Help

It's not easy to ask for help, is it? We wander around this plane trying to figure out who we are, getting stuck here or there, not knowing what to do next. We are hampered by this unwillingness to seek help.

"Who can do it alone?" we could ask. Well, no one, apparently. We all rely on each other at some level. There are days when we feel strong and days when we feel weak. Leaning on each other is a requisite to getting by in this life. Culture can say what it wants about "doing it alone" or that "men are stronger than women." The fact is we need each other in times of weakness and it doesn't matter what gender steps up to lend a hand.

When we are too tired or ill to do it ourselves, we need to reach out and take that hand, to let someone help and pull us free of the swamp. Better than drowning, isn't it? Better than giving up altogether.

Sometimes life shows us things we need to learn in the smaller problems we face. We may believe they are huge, but perhaps they are merely instructive, designed to push us out of a certain impasse. Oh sure, we'd rather read the book; that would be easier. But some lessons have to be earned. They have to be taken through life experience because they require more than mere intellectual appreciation.

It's difficult, though, those times we feel overwhelmed by one of life's challenges. Yes, we'd rather walk around that swamp and study it from a distance, than wade our way through and get dirty. That's when help may be required, when the challenge feels too tough to manage alone. So ask! Someone will come along and offer you a hand. Take it! Don't be shy. And don't be apologetic. You weren't designed to do everything by yourself.

5 – How We Lost Our Way

The heroic quest is an adventure, unbridled and true. It moves one from the past to the present and into the future, always pointing the way to a new destination. We will see this unfold as we move along with this review.

The myths of the world typically say one thing; God is alive and well, and lives in our hearts. Our task is to find the God energy within ourselves. God is no longer out there in some church, some doctrine or similar external authority. These sources cannot provide all that we need today. God, the Great Creator, resides within each and every one of us and that force animates all life as we experience it. Every living creature, every entity that breathes and gives off energy is of the God force. We are God, individually and collectively. We wander this planet in search of our individualized God nature to reveal our piece of this great cosmic puzzle.

How did we get turned away from this all important purpose, this destiny we charted, this pursuit of Self, Soul and love as the ultimate frontier? How did we become so lost in the desert of a constricted and displaced emotional life that we began wandering aimlessly? How, for so many centuries, have we strayed so far away from our own true nature?

In the stories of creation, of which there are many varieties, it is said that man was an experiment and God observed with great joy how our lives played out and how we met our needs. Later, it was said that humans, as creatures, were viewed as so beautiful that the "Gods" wanted to co-mingle with humanity. This began the descent into matter, into the density of the planet, into the roots of the material world. This was the beginning of the trance. Like the director who believes his movie is real life rather than a metaphor, we lost sight of our Divine inheritance when we fell into the belief that earth life was all there was. There have been many movies about this subject, where someone loses their way in a self-created reality, forgetting they have the keys to a much nobler destiny.

The symbolism of myth eloquently captures this hypnotic state. Heroes are always typically cast into situations they must overcome to resume their lives and retrieve some treasure. Gold is not the treasure--love is! Love of life, the earth, one's fellow man and love of mystery are the real treasures. Most certainly the love of the mystery of life!

We are taught as children that magic and mystery exist, but cannot be fully understood. Most world religions like to underline the fact that magic and mystery are fathomless. This type of teaching has been continued by self-appointed spiritualists who have become mired in their self-created matrix. The whole notion is absurd. When you're always looking outside of yourself, following formulas and scripts, you inevitably lose your way. The lesson from both myth and modern therapy is to look within.

Children don't believe that magic and mystery are fathomless until they are taught this and conditioned to the idea. At this point, they turn off their curious quest. Intuitively they know that God, something greater than themselves, exists in their hearts. They believe the mystery is solvable, if only someone would help them understand it. Our God nature certainly knows this to be true. The Creator placed this key inside all our hearts. Our challenge is to retrieve it for ourselves. This quest is particularly challenging because we have been conditioned away from the process.

Heroism is about working our way back to that core center through our feelings, emotions and our very human nature. We are sentient beings who have a heart center to guide us. We can learn to trust this resource early in life when demonstrated by others already on the quest. All children are budding artists. With their heart center easily available, they are ready to bloom with our encouragement. This native ability can equally be squashed with rigid dogma originating from external sources and rigid 3rd dimensional thinking.

It is sad that recent generations, including our own, have contributed to this process of not trusting the Self. This is how we lost our way. This is how gods become mere mortals with nowhere to turn except where egos point. And egos, as history repeatedly demonstrates, are ill equipped to guide gods forward.

This is how it all began. We literally forgot that we were the gods who set out on this mortal journey. We fell in love with our creations, the material body and earthly circumstances, and lost our "Self" in the process. When we finally woke up we began to realize we had created the life drama we were caught in. We are not yet fully awake, but we are becoming more conscious of this fact than ever before.

The Army of Light is waking from its slumber, reaching for greater illumination, greater levels of awareness, while moving ahead with grand purpose and design. Everywhere heroes and heroines are charting their path Home. Remember the fine familiar phrase, "Home is where the heart is." We can re-assert this with authority when we remember its true meaning.

What do such phrases mean for a population gone mad, being so far removed from its original purpose? It means we are fighting our way back, en masse, to the pulsating heart center, where the divine pulse of the Creator resides and animates our lives, where Souls sing in harmony and play together like a well-rehearsed symphony. That's how the Army of Light works, in sync with all parts of itself, fully informed and fully alive. Every instrument pulsates to its own tempo and is, yet, synchronized with the whole orchestra.

How do we get there, to this ideal we fashion and project onto the movie screen of our lives? What is required of us to make this happen? We must listen! We must learn! We must act! When we hear our inner voice we must listen and move with it. Let it guide the way. Listen to the Voice, the Soul, the only beacon worthy of note, the message created and installed by God. We move forward as directed and we find our way home.

In the coming chapters we will look more closely at this activation process, this inner guidance and how it functions in our lives. There are many seekers who are actively engaged in this process today, directing their lives from their respective centers. We will examine how they arrived at this point and flesh out the process in greater detail. The answers we seek are as intriguing as the questions.

The answers beg for greater understanding and take us deeper into the heart of the mystery, the place we were forbidden to enter as children. As adults, we can move beyond the indoctrination we received as children. Now, we can boldly go into the heart of the mystery. No one can hold us back any longer - no institution, no religion, and no authority outside of us. We are the masters of our destiny. Our questions will take us where we need to go!

Fear

What is it about fear that gets us all tied up in knots? Is it the biological realm rearing its head in the face of a possible threat? Is it our minds making mountains out of molehills? Or is it some other nefarious element that lies outside of our control? The "fight or flight" response says you must make a choice, based on what's in front of you and what capacity you believe you have to deal with it.

It's not always right, this "fight or flight" response. Sometimes we act when leaving would be a better option. Sometimes we stay to quickly learn that was inadvisable. So how do we deal with fear in a manner that is most compatible with our True Self?

The nature of fear is twofold. First, we are reacting to a real or perceived danger. Second, there is an urge to do something about it, be it magical or otherwise. For a physical danger, fight or flight is likely the best course of action. We measure the danger and act, by either removing ourselves or confronting it.

With perceived danger it's an entirely different matter. Here we are manufacturing fear in response to a threat elicited in our minds. There may be a real trigger involved, but it's what we do with it that takes us toward denial and/or paralysis. We now have an unspoken fear that we will attempt to manage with food, alcohol or other distractions.

It is rarely enough to realize that we are fearful and then choose to do something about it. It is exacting and true, however, that when we address the feeling of fear, we can get past it. What is necessary is that we accept it, let it flow through us and let it be. But when we run, hide, gesticulate or attempt to annihilate, we inevitably fail because these measures hide the real truth about fear. It's a feeling! We need to accept it and feel it before we can release it.

Feel it! Love it! Embrace it! And fear will move through you. Fight it and you become its prisoner. So follow the path of accepting the fear as your own and then release it when you no longer need it. The lesson is learned. You can let it go. It is simple and effective. Try it and see for yourself.

6 – The Big Sleep

The heart of life's mystery is within us and we are within it. The orchestra warms up to play the overture. We take a deep breath. We exhale. The God within us jumps up and the music begins.

Imagine an orchestra leader and band members forgetting where they are in the musical performance and what to play next. "What am I supposed to do?" they might ask, feeling bewildered and confused, holding a magnificent instrument that is theirs alone and not knowing what to do with it. This is a reflection of who we are at this point in history, looking around, wondering what to do next. The maestro taps the podium. What are you to do? What do any of us do?

We take up the challenge and move forward, that's what we do. We learn our parts. We jump in. We play our song. We make our contribution to the whole. But, we forgot, didn't we? How do we get back to our place? How do we learn to play our part again? That is the question we will answer now.

Long ago, when our race was younger, we lost our way. People turned away from their heart center and truest path to focus on survival. Survival, at that time, meant giving up our Self. At that time humans were being battered by numerous forces that included meeting basic survival needs while dealing with dysfunctional authorities who did not know how to provide healthy modeling and direction. Many set their selves aside in favor of more pressing realities such as getting through life each day while trying to make sense of so many conflicting directives.

Our parents were lost as well, having inherited from the previous generation the conflicting directives espoused by church authorities and governments of the time. The roots of this disorder have been referred to as "The Fall." And that is when the Big Sleep overcame a majority of humanity. Before, we humans were in regular touch with the Creator and could access our own divinity whenever we focused within. We knew the Creator did not sit on Mount Olympus, as some stories would have it. At some level, we were still aware that the Creator traveled with us, as one of us. For example, Jesus' task was to reawaken the population to that truth, but he was misunderstood and idolized. Jesus came to tell everyone that they were just like him, able to call upon all the truths of life in this world and know these in their hearts.

Jesus said "You shall do wonders greater than these," referring to what was considered extraordinary, turning water into wine and raising the dead, as examples. These were quite marvelous feats but then so is levitating a body or pulling a rabbit out of a hat as many of today's magicians are able to do. Jesus was not a trickster, but rather a carrier of the truth. And that truth was that everyone carried the truth. This very important truth, which is ours to begin with, is manifested in the metaphors of Jesus' teachings. It is every person's task to uncover that truth, dust it off and share it with the world.

Today, we have an information explosion. The internet, newspapers and electronic media connect us to every part of the world and to every source of both useful and not so useful information we could ever desire. Yet, many lives remain unfulfilled and devoid of personal meaning. Very little of this information actually resonates with our truth, our reality, our piece of the cosmic puzzle. Much sifting of this information tsunami is required to discern something of value. Much of it, as we well know, is simple disinformation issued for the purpose of advancing some authority's agenda.

I have referred to this truth we are seeking as the Golden Truth, the pulse that animates all life, our Heart and our Souls. These are symbols for an inner reality that connects us with All-That-Is, the Great Creator, the Inner Voice. This inner reality is the key to who we are. Our feelings, our

Heart and our Souls take us there. We are truth and we are God in this realm. Let us choose to awaken and retrieve that reality for ourselves.

We were lulled to sleep as children. More accurately, we were conditioned to the dominant trance of our culture. In part, this happened because our parents looked to us to fill their hungry hearts which were left wanting by their emotionally distant parents who never had all their needs met either. This cycle of feeding off the young for one's emotional fulfillment perpetuated this symbiotic cycle and kept the population trapped in this interminable sleep. This emotional hunger keeps us looking for comfort outside ourselves while our connection to the Divine goes unattended. The responsibility for breaking this cycle has now shifted to us.

At this time in history, there is a growing impetus to challenge the old rule and return to our roots which are our divine heritage. This is the place where we can no longer be enslaved because we all belong to God. God is us, and that is the plain and simple truth. Healing ourselves will take us there. We need to trust ourselves, to see and believe that this power we seek has always been ours. It was through a certain misfortune of circumstances and adaptations in previous generations that we lost our way.

When you learn to trust yourself and recognize that this is your correct path, you cannot be enslaved again. You can only belong to the Creator who gave you life and invited you on this journey of self-exploration and self-discovery, and urged you to cross the mountains and plains of the earth and move into the hills and valleys of your heart. "Come play with me" the Creator said, "and I will join you there. Don't forget who I am now, and certainly don't forget who you are," was likely added.

There is a movement afoot to affirm who we are, who we truly are. As we undo the misdirection that enslaved us over the past several centuries, we return to that center within, the place where the Self turns on its axis and shows us our part in this grand design.

We are now here at the threshold we must cross, the one predicted by the soothsayers and prophets of years gone by. From seers like Nostradamus to great poets like William Shakespeare, from Walt Whitman to Bob Dylan, from Buddha to the Dalai Lama, they remind us of the same reality, that there is only one truth that lights up our lives. Christ, God, Mohammed or Krishna lives and is here among us, rising right now in the throng we call The Army of Light. We are here and the Creator is among us. There is nothing but joy to be had in this knowledge.

We now realize that there is no savior per se, only us saving ourselves. We are the answer to our prayers. Our twelve step groups, our spiritual growth classes, our meditation exercises, our New Age studies, whatever calls us, commands our attention and draws us inward can be a way out of our sleep. Whatever alerts us to the world within and without, whatever places us in the therapist's office or a support group is our challenge to heed and our path to follow. This is our goal friends, to find our one true path and see it to the end. We can no longer shut out our heart-centered lives. Healing our wounds will set us free. I believe that with all my heart and I've dedicated my life to it.

As we ponder this next horizon, we ask ourselves how we get there. The repression of previous generations that denied us our emotional and feeling reality can no longer restrain us. We moved beyond this particular stumbling block toward the healing movements that are currently afoot, helping people recover hope, confront childhood traumas and deal with similar blockages. What is the essence of all these healing thrusts? We will examine that now.

When therapists take clients on to their caseload there is one primary purpose—assist this person in overcoming the blockages to their evolution at the moment. Initially, it may not look like this, their problem having been tagged as a phobia, work trauma, parental intrusion or other psychological infraction, but that is what it is. We evolve more or less naturally with healthy parenting and mentoring. When these processes go awry, we become blocked. With the right kind of help we become unblocked and return to our natural path. That is when we continue to evolve. Perhaps clumsily at first, but certainly more consciously now that our inner guidance is leading the way.

At this time in our collective human history, we, as a species, can choose. We can embrace Conscious Evolution or we can remain unconscious and continue stumbling along in concert with our unexamined life script. The latter has been the unspoken and unchallenged status quo until now, while the former is the newly articulated spiritual path many of us are choosing to follow. Major aspects of a New Age psychology and spiritual awareness are focused on Conscious Evolution. The New Age has given us some great resource material. But aspects of this movement do nothing more than identify the current fad and try to capitalize on it. This false application of evolving ideas will not have any longevity. The true path attracts truth seekers who are thoughtful and responsible and approach this newly emerging material with discernment.

Conscious Evolution is exactly that, becoming conscious of who we are, what we feel and think, and taking full responsibility for ourselves. We can no more deny this to ourselves than we can stop our breathing. It is a fact of our lives. Becoming awake means we become responsible and fully alive, experiencing both the pain and the ecstasy of life's freedom when lived consciously.

When we first attempted to shut out life's pain, we immediately became enslaved to it. Caught in its grip we writhed and twisted in a desperate attempt to set ourselves free. But, we couldn't because we had shut off access to our center, our feeling network, our heart, the place where everything is processed. Without this center of feeling activity to guide us we became lost. Many offered us their brand of salvation. No brand would ever work, unless it included a route back to our Self. In our center of experience is where the damage lay and needed correcting. This is where the psychological and emotional blows first took place and knocked us off course. These injuries would stay within, buried, but active, until we owned them and took responsibility to work our way through them.

Psychological and emotional wounds have an uncanny ability to deny time. The fact that they occurred many years ago is irrelevant. Emotional wounds know nothing of time, they continue to fester and drive us. We are speaking of unhealed wounds that have kept us stuck. There is no absence of woundedness within our lives. There is only an absence of healing.

Our unhealed wounds threw us off course. Those injuries are what need to be addressed in the present. Otherwise, they continue to exist unhealed. Through my years of practice, I worked with many adults, male and female, who were beginning to remember childhood sexual abuse decades after it had occurred. Those marks were as fresh as the day they were inflicted and their wounded heart closed up. Such woundedness keeps us from our Self until we find the courage to go within, to the scene of the damage, and repair the original rupture. Many of us need to undertake this mission.

I had many cases like this during my years of practice. It frequently happened that someone would show up at my office recounting a recurrent dream or repeating behavior pattern that kept them stuck in some quagmire, be that low self-esteem, anxiety or depression. Oftentimes, these wounds were wrapped in guilt and shame. These people were at war with themselves without knowing why. An injured part of them was trying to get their attention and another part them kept trying to push a memory away, judging it as old, frightening or irrelevant.

After an initial assessment, it was explained to the client that this war would continue unless their approach changed, unless they listened to the feeling memory and understood what it was trying to tell them. After realizing that I was not going to align with their unhealthy protector Self, the part of them that wanted to continue denying their experiences, they would finally accept that they had to go through these feelings, and I would guide them along. Through the process of accepting and feeling their pain, they learned that therapy was safe and it brought with it increased emotional freedom.

Working through feelings is exactly like this. These have to be accepted before we can finally move forward and bring more consciousness into our evolution. As repressed feelings began to be released, using the tools of acceptance and emotional expression, the client would see for themselves that this was the better alternative, one they could apply to many dimensions of their life experience. They were no longer at odds with themselves by rejecting what needed to be heard. By listening to those inner voices, and accepting and moving through their blocked feelings proved to be the better option.

As clients began accepting and listening to their feeling nature, they were typically moved to tears. They often felt a strong urge to forgive themselves for their contributions of self-criticism and self-denigration. They could end the cycle of replicating what they had learned from unhealthy authority figures. The role I played in my clients' lives was that of ally, mentor and supporter. Therapy ended when they adopted and incorporated those roles for themselves.

This explains why so few of us can do transformation on our own. In fact, none of us really do. We don't all necessarily go to a support group or seek the assistance of a therapist, but we do talk to friends, write in journals or visit a talk show that addresses our problem. We all suffer in similar ways, especially when we are closed up. We feel as if the world is doing something to us when we are in fact recycling those original traumatic circumstances and the associated feelings. We repeat such behavior until we find the right help and learn a better way.

No one moves forward psychologically, spiritually or emotionally until their state of woundedness has been accepted and healed. This process of acceptance is at the heart of Conscious Evolution. Choosing to heal ourselves by uncovering our unconscious blockages is the first step.

Choosing our brand of emotional and spiritual growth is the next step on the horizon.

Secrets

What are those deep dark secrets that we keep to ourselves? Are they the soundings of some distant past trying to break through into our current reality? The voice of reason perhaps, wanting to cut across the chatter that is our brain feverishly at work? Or, is it something else altogether, so remote and bizarre that we can't even fathom it with the best of detailed roadmaps?

Is this our heritage knocking at the door? Is it a source of pride perhaps, or a bit of whimsy? All these possibilities exist in one form or another. They are real to those who attend to them. But to us who are waking up to something meaningful and deep, is it not possible that the Creator is knocking at the door and we are about to receive a very important message?

"Remember when I sent you here. Remember our agreement. I provide the resources and you provide the commitment. We work together to elevate your life to a new plateau, so that others can see what is possible."

A formidable calling, is it not? Throughout history there have been claims like this, but so many were false. Soothsayers and prophets asserted they were inside the Creator's mind in one form or another. We know these characters and how they were shown the door by their own impatience and claims to fame. We've seen them in our own era.

We are not talking about that kind of false awakening. We are talking about something real and tenable: The rise of the Force within us; the birth of Christ through us. As myth would suggest, the arrival of the Holy Self on a chariot with winged horses.

Yes, we're talking about the kind of revelation that leaves you gasping for air and wondering if you've just been electrocuted. That's the kind of awakening that's coming your way now. We want the real thing, all the experiences and feelings, including the fear that we can now accept.

There it is, the message delivered to us. Are we ready for this? It will be exciting! Hang on tight as we explore the 5th dimension.

7 – Conscious Evolution

Conscious Evolution is now a fact of life. No one can deny that. All around us there is evidence of this new reality taking root. Barbara Marx Hubbard, along with other thought leaders such as Eckhart Tolle and Mark Allen, have been pointing toward the social context of this revolution. In our school systems, for example, we have seen drastic changes. What was once unheard of is now common place. Sex education, conflict resolution, emotional literacy, all of these and more have risen to the forefront. Child preparedness for unseen dangers and greater awareness of one's environment are daily staples. The three Rs remain the same, but the social context of a child's life has been expanded and broadened to meet our growing understanding of their needs.

Young children know where babies come from. Adults share their life experiences to help children better understand their own. Police officers and fireman are not the only attraction at school assemblies. Speakers from Al-Anon and other twelve step programs have made much appreciated appearances. So have representatives from groups such as Parents without Partners, public health and drug and alcohol educators. These and more have offered valuable information to help students see their lives in a larger context.

Children are asked how they feel now, not just what they think. They are receiving instruction on how to handle their emotions and on how to express themselves without violence. We have clearly traveled some distance from that generation who grew up in silence, who was not allowed to feel and was seriously condemned when they did. Conscious Evolution is here and has taken root in today's culture. We don't have to look far to see it in all of our lives, not just those of our children.

What does this mean for us as individuals? How does one engage in this process? We begin with a scenario, one that is all too common these days. A woman comes to a therapist's office to discuss sexual abuse. She thinks it happened during childhood, but she's not sure. All her life, as far back as she can remember, she's had a recurring dream. A man comes to her and asks her for a favor. He wants her to hold a stick for him while he massages her feet. She wakes up in a sweat, her mind whirling with the images. What does this dream mean? Why does she fear it? Why, for so many years, has it kept recurring? Lately, a few twists have been added to the dream. The man has an eerie smile. He looks at her as if he wants to devour her. She feels helpless and frozen. She fears the massage and the stick. As she slowly becomes untangled, she realizes what these symbols mean. He wants to touch her genitals. He wants her to touch him in the same way. "It's all right," he says, "no one will ever know." She feels sick to her stomach and wants to throw up. She can't stand the dream anymore. She's feeling panic. She suspects sexual abuse but can't believe that it is possible. But it is!

She hears one expert after another, on television, radio and in the press, discussing this very topic with themes that are already too familiar. They reveal that one in three females and one in four males have been victims of childhood sexual abuse. She also hears that many incidents of abuse have never been reported. She realizes the odds are high and sinks into a depression. She begins to seriously consider that this may be true for her.

Her girlfriend suggests she see a therapist, which our dreamer reluctantly agrees to do. The therapist helps her address her worst fears. All the signs are there. She is urged to check within and ask herself "does it feel true?" "Yes," she asserts and then breaks into tears, looking totally bewildered and devastated. Her body shakes with the realization. Her defenses crack and crumble. "What do I do now?" she asks. "You work it through," is the reply. "I will help you" the therapist continues. "Here are some books to read that lay out a path we can follow together. You will get through this. I will be right there beside you every step of the way and for as long as you need me."

The devastating realization sinks in. "I am a victim of childhood sexual abuse. Oh my God, what am I going to do?" "Breathe," the therapist urges. "Don't forget to breathe." And here we have the beginnings of a process which repeats itself thousands of times a day as men and women everywhere come to grips with childhood sexual abuse and the great variety of similar traumas that have left an indelible mark on their psyche.

Throughout history there has never been a shortage of such abuses and traumas. The difference is that today people are willing and wanting to confront these issues, and there is help available for them. Victims no longer hide in shame and hope the traumatic images and memories will just go away. People are now aware that will never happen, and they are willing to share their stories with others.

This is what we are seeing around us, on television, radio talk shows and autobiographical stories. People are opening up and revealing their truth. One's woundedness is completely acceptable as a topic for discussion. Once they have embarked on that path, we know they have taken evolution into their own hands, and made it a conscious process. And that's the way it goes, this active pursuit of self-acceptance and forgiveness for one's abusers. One's devotion to the truth and pursuit of true freedom is undertaken no matter what the cost.

You don't have to know everything to make life work. What you must know is how to get what you need. Once you know this, you can manage any eventuality. The conspiracy of silence that has dominated our culture for so many generations now goes the way of the dinosaur. This pattern is relegated to a dark past of our history, the last vestiges of the "era of sleep" that we are now exiting. Conscious Evolution has staked its claim and is being accepted as the new wave. Our God nature is at work moving us forward and preparing us for the changes ahead. Those who bemoan the new era in favor of the silence of the past are stuck and will remain behind.

Every era has had its proponents and its holdouts and both groups ultimately contribute to the changes taking a firm hold.

Now we move to another subject. One that affects us all and leaves us bewildered at the same time. I am speaking of our relationship to God, the Great Creator, the Energy that animates us all. If the process of evolution is becoming more conscious, then how does God fit into the picture? It might seem absurd to us that a Creator would actually ever lose sight of its God nature. But that is precisely what has happened to us as Gods in the human body.

We started out as God wanting to experiment in one of the Universe's many playgrounds, but we lost sight of our origins during the unfolding of our earthly drama. Now, we are seeking to retrieve ourselves. This was not part of the original plan as I understand it, but we fell asleep, nevertheless. We are now proceeding on a course that requires us to participate consciously as masters of our own fate.

To retrieve our God Self, we must go inward. If I am the Source of greatness and abundance, then there is only one place to look for that which I misplaced. That is what the woman unveiling sexual abuse is doing. She is looking inward. She is not looking for her God Self at first glance, but eventually that is what she will find. Her woundedness will lead her to that lost treasure. The original wound and her subsequent repression closed her off from that reality when it became cloaked in defenses. But the wound in need of healing will take her back to that rupture. She will retrieve what was lost as she sticks to her healing journey. Recovery books of every stripe tell us so. All the twelve-step programs are imbued with this very premise.

God works in mysterious ways. Well yes, maybe. But what is so mysterious about looking inward? Whenever anything malfunctions, we look inside to see what is happening, don't we? We need to understand how it works to understand the malfunction. Our human psychology and emotional functioning can be understood through the intent to move inward.

That which animates us is completely fathomable if we pursue that avenue of inquiry. Addictions and similar defensive strategies keep us from asking these questions. Defenses will crumble once they are challenged.

It would appear that we live in one of the most addictive times in human history. It begs the question - what are we so afraid of? I believe it is psychological and emotional pain. Dealing with this pain keeps many wounded people away from the help they need. Governments make millions of dollars offering products and services that help keep us numb. They supply us with major distractions and keep us coming back for more. Alcohol, coffee, cigarettes, gambling, all government controlled and subsidized. Ironically, these revenues are used to assist the very population that they first sought to seduce. Here we have a vicious circle. We have the choice, we know that, but many of us still fall prey to one or more of these addictions, especially during times of vulnerability when our wounds are causing distress.

We would do well to understand this process of addiction and numbing out through these distractions that are socially sanctioned and government supported. The vicious cycle turns again, and now we have wars on drugs and all their toxic counterparts. We focus on everything except the real problem in these situations, which includes our hungry hearts and our Souls yearning for nourishment. Such a war should not be against the substance or process of addiction. There will always be more of these substances, and we imbue them with too much power. Illegal drugs aside, socially sanctioned prescription medications and gambling facilities can take us into their grip and enslave us just as well. They are not the culprit, nor are the governments, big business or organized crime, all of whom are capitalizing on these weaknesses. The problem lies within us, our woundedness and our separation from the Self and our divine aspect.

A state of grace does not have to be legislated or purchased. It is free! Look inward! Look inward and find your true Self waiting to be acknowledged. This is the journey consistently depicted in every hero myth; the quest, the struggle and the enlightenment.

We are preparing for a major leap forward in our evolution, one that requires our conscious participation. There is no doubt of that. As we look forward to this emerging millennium, we must ask ourselves – for what is it that we hope? We no longer want denial, addiction and unconscious fumbling. We want something different this time, something radically different.

Not a utopia, but a conscious pilgrimage to the center of our being, a well-worn and discernible path to God. No frills, no extras, no fancy affairs. I want a full-fledged embrace of the Divine within me and all the healing that this choice can muster. We desperately need this now. We need to go forward, and this is the path to follow. We cannot fail when guided by the Divine that lives within each of us. God's neighborhood is the human heart, our feeling center. We will not find this center at a church, synagogue or temple. We will find it in our heart, at the center of our being. That Divine aspect is ours to retrieve. And I believe that is why we are here.

We are at the threshold of a new era, one that requires our conscious participation. We can no longer afford to be pushed and prodded by life in a seemingly random and aimless fashion. By taking hold of ourselves, we can change the course of our destiny, and that of the planet. Imagine being on a bus and not knowing where it is going. That would be unacceptable. We need to know where we are going and have some say in how the journey is to proceed. The journey is the destination.

Grace and Glory

Glory belongs to the passing era of competition and conquest, when our spiritual lives didn't seem to matter as much as they do now. In *Grace*, we are pointed in a whole new direction where the Self comes to surface and takes us onto a new path toward spiritual wholeness.

As we are guided toward this mission of mercy, we realize that others' needs are equal to our own. We are advised that anything is possible, but not as determined by fate as we once thought. We have choice in all matters, conscious choice.

Where we take this *Grace* is up to us at this juncture. We can overdo it as we did with *Glory* in our past. Or we can take a new tack and discover something miraculous about ourselves. We are truly capable of helping one another, through our respective challenges and we can deliver this assistance with compassion. We can open to a whole new way of being, not measured by what *Glory* used as standards for success.

In these new ventures inward, we will find our Self; this lively pulse within which calls to us. It announces the advent of a new era, one that is governed by the quality of the heart and no longer by the statistics of accumulation and conquest.

Yes, we have defenses. But do we need them now? It's time to let go of outworn postures and make room for a new way of relating to ourselves. Is *Glory* worth pursuing, or should we abandon it like so many exhausted adventures?

It's time to open up now and heal that wounded dove that is our Self. To set it free upon the winds of time and see what *Graces* are there to be won?

Then so be it. Let it begin!

8 – The Force

Conscious Evolution is now a common reference in the personal growth literature with many well-known proponents actively discussing it on the lecture circuit. Everywhere there are signs that more and more people are on that path. Talk shows present us with such individuals every day and the aisles of New Age book stores are filled with the latest releases addressing this multifaceted subject. It would seem that the God of Heaven wishes to be known at this time and the necessary reference material has been brought down to Earth for all to see. This God knows no bounds and will stop at nothing to be known, wanting you and me, all of us, to be aware of the one truth that really matters. We are not forsaken, we are not lost, only misguided, closed off from our true selves and sidelined for the moment.

We are making our way back, bit by bit, step by step. We are finding our way to center again. In the last chapter we addressed the issue of Conscious Evolution through the woman who was a victim of sexual abuse. She exemplifies what so many of us are called to do, open to our Self and find our way Home through the pain and hardship of healing inner wounds , as is necessary when we are guarded with defenses that no longer work.

Many of us have chosen this path of recovery through pain, not consciously, at least not initially. But if we set the stage for these events that drove us to recovery, then we did indeed make a conscious choice at some point. But that is another matter.

Choosing to heal is the first step in the current affair, the matter of engaging Conscious Evolution on this plane of existence. Healing does not occur in a vacuum. It always takes place in concert with others. We seek each other out in supportive environments. We go to the therapist's office or join AA, we take a weekend retreat or head for the bookstore, we look to each other for guidance and support; we comfort each other with well chose words. We hide in silence only occasionally now to temporarily retreat from the work. Then, we return to the fray again and again, until it is done, until this healing process is complete.

Why do we do this? Is it the promise of a better life? Is it a further deadening of the pain? Is it a conscious choice to pursue retribution or vengeance? The motives aren't the same throughout the process. These change at different stages. Suffice it to say, we are driven, and what drives us is that Force, that inalienable Force that brought us here in the first place. That Force is dynamic, it wants to live, and wants to move forward. That Force is not satisfied with mere existence. It wants much more than healing from this earthly life.

How is it that we keep that Force in check for such a long time before we finally surrender to its deepest motives? It is inalienable. It seduces us. It draws us inward to our secret selves where the damage first manifested, where we covered up and ran, where we tried our best to escape. This is how powerful such a Force can be. No mere pretence, denial or defense system will ever keep it submerged indefinitely. This is not possible. This is too powerful a motive to ever be held back indefinitely.

We can hold this Force down for some time, but not forever. Forever extends beyond this lifetime into the next and the one after that. This Force does not give up, never dies and never goes away. It urges us to keep coming at a problem until we master it. This Force both drives and supports us all. "To where?" we might ask, "and for what purpose?"

We are breathless at the thought. But the mind of God is no trickster. It knows exactly what it wants: a man, a woman, a child in happy comfort and blooming year round. We were created that way, to bloom again and again. Only our defenses and respective fears get in the way. And fear is the sine qua non of aversion to growth. Growth demands a confrontation with fear.

Again we are returned to the Myth of the Hero. What is it that the hero overcomes, but fear? That is the quest after all, repeating itself in scenario after scenario, century after century, all the way forward to the present from further back than we can remember. From cave drawings to textbooks, we are reminded that this has always been part of the human quest, to retrieve that lost Golden Self and have fear overturned in the process.

Some of the worst fears to be confronted are those from childhood, those that came too quickly before we were prepared to deal with life. For some of us, these early traumas occurred in the crib and left their telltale mark from the very beginning of this incarnation. Why would we choose such a horrible beginning? Only the hero or heroine of that particular drama can ever know. Those answers are written within each person's heart.

Such challenges are set in motion before we incarnate. We laid out this path of experience knowing full well we would succumb to the Big Sleep that was current in the human experience. Each of us who stepped into this realm at that particular time took that step consciously, then arrived here to forget the process altogether. Yet where would we be if some force or energy didn't move us along? This is the Life Force that nudges us, pushes us, and prods us into seeking the help and circumstances we need to begin our healing journeys. Many of us have found our way due mainly to this Force. It would appear we are never completely asleep after all.

Each time a truth arises from within, we recognize it immediately. This is the "ah hah" experience. Some internal reference point says that's true, for me at least. That's what our woman said earlier when she recognized sexual abuse. She had one of these experiences, an internal reverberation that said this information was true for her. As she looks into her void she will find many more "ah hahs" and they will signal she's on the right path and nudge her to where she needs to go. Her therapist is her guide. She is on the journey!

This is what happens to so many stepping onto this trail. Looking through the scattered rubble of our dysfunctional beginnings, we find bits and pieces that reverberate with this inner knowing, a felt note that says "this is true for me." This is how we all learn. Without that note where would we be?

Our great debate is not about what's true, but rather what "feels" true. Your truth is not essentially the same as mine, although we do share truth. There are, after all, common denominators in truth. We will strike similar chords with each other now and then, that is inevitable.

We gather in groups to share those common truths, to learn from each other, to support one another. That is how truth leaps from one Soul to the next. By recognition! By transference! By striking a familiar vibration! We hear these echoes from each other as they circulate the globe, leaping from Heart to Heart, Soul to Soul. We see God in action as we come closer to recognizing our similarities which, in turn, minimize our differences. We are not so dissimilar after all, even when we come from entirely different origins—culturally, philosophically or otherwise.

This is how it goes, this process of upheaval and change. Round and round it turns, until we take charge of our lives. We learn from each other. This is absolutely so. How else is it to be since we are cut from the same Divine cloth?

Where does this process go from here, after the healing journey? That's the new territory some might call utopia. But utopia is an ideal without change or challenge. An entity that wants to grow will want to be challenged. Where do we proceed after the healing journey? Many of us are still riveted to the healing side of this process and can't see what lies ahead. For now, trusting the Force and listening to our Heart is all that is required.

"What if God were one of us?" a contemporary song asks. God is a part of us as we are of God. As such God wants each of us to move along on our respective journey. And this is tricky. A man or woman in the midst of a struggle to heal his or her wounded Self has a purpose and a goal. They stay fixed on it until they get to the end. But then what? The person who pursued healing was wounded and healing that woundedness is what defined them for the length of that process. But who are they now that the healing has taken place?

These healed individuals are someone else now. If they are no longer defined by their wounds, then who are they? Where will they want to go now that the healing is finished? Many of us are arriving at this point in our lives. What lies ahead over the next horizon, around that corner or through the next door? We don't know for certain. In the meantime, we speculate. God will inform us through our desires and inner attractions when the time is right. We will be shown where we might go next.

In the next chapter we will look at what comes beyond the healing. This is the next stage in our Conscious Evolution. Where might this take us?

Receiving

Receiving is a generous gift to us. Our Soul says "open and I will pour love into you." Love from God, it appears, which is abundant and most satisfying.

It is said that only animals and small children know how to receive. It's a natural state for them, completely instinctual it would seem. What happens to us on our way to adulthood? How do we learn to shut out that ever flowing fountain of gifts from God the Creator?

Something happens when we become obsessed with making it alone and trying to control the flow of good into our lives. This is fear at work. Fear says you have to do it all by yourself. Love says "come back to me and I will show you how to reopen that heart so you can once again receive." Re-engaging this native tendency now has to be a choice.

Perhaps the lesson is this: We are naturally capable of receiving and enjoying the bounty that God and Life have to offer. To deny ourselves these benefits, we actually have to "learn" to close up. This is the essence of the "Fall." We fall from God's grace into turmoil by believing that all suffering is bad and we must close off these feelings in order to be safe. Cutting off our suffering means we are cut off from Source as well.

Redemption comes through surrender. By surrendering, we open up and release those so-called safety defenses. Then we regain our capacity to receive. In so doing, we become vulnerable. In this life there are losses and heartaches to grieve alongside receiving that which is good for us. Life is both bitter and sweet. Only by accepting this and surrendering to God's grace do we return to that primal reality, where we know life will renew us after every round of difficulty.

Now we are adults, not children anymore. And we know life can be bittersweet in spite of that loving connection to the Great Creator. We accept that reality at this juncture because we have grown. We know what it's like to be closed off from the Creator's love. We now choose to be the embodiment of that love. The suffering passes.

It always does. The reign of love remains constant and waits patiently for our return. Reach out and grab it; it belongs to you.

9 – Beyond Healing

The healing journey sits behind us now as we look to the horizon to see what's coming next. Many of us are standing on this hill right now, marching toward the future eager to see what comes up for us. How exciting!

We are eager and scared at the same time. The healing journey gave our life perspective and a set of references to which we could relate. Books were passed around, workshops and seminars were attended, and journal writing was completed. We pursued all manner of inner explorations designed to bring healing to that wounded part within. We knew where we were then. That particular framework surrounded us and gave us comfort. Now we are standing at a new frontier, one that's not well charted, defined or laid out, one that leaves us trembling as we contemplate our next step.

Here we reach back to myth once again. What did the hero and heroine do at this point in their journey? How did they serve their fellow man? What was the nature of their blossoming? What will be the nature of your own?

Myth teaches us that all eventualities are cyclical. After any one phase is completed, there comes another, and then another, all succeeding each other in a well-orchestrated sequence. Beginnings, middles and endings, all following each other as surely as the cycles of the moon, the turning of the planets and the movements of the stars, each remaining true to some guiding principle that never fails in its measured and predictable unfolding. What goes around comes around. What follows one, follows all.

Some would call this idea a utopia, but that is not so. Utopia is the word we use for the fantasy concept of perfection. Perfection does not exist in our dualistic material world. Only the ego with its many defensive strategies holds on to the illusion of utopia. The position we are talking about is a stance toward life, one that sees us consciously aware of our inner driving force, the native energy that lights our path and guides us forward.

After the healing journey, there is truth. The truth that the God energy, our inner referent, is what leads the way from here. We can dispute this if we wish. We can engage in endless philosophical arguments, but the truth is still the truth. God resides within, we are God and it is this Force which will lead the way from this point. This means we must surrender control, or more accurately, the illusion of control. Conscious Evolution leads to God.

So what does it mean to be led by God? Does it mean we no longer have free will? Not at all! We are free to choose as always. But why would we choose a path that takes us away from God when being God is all there is? Does that mean that God's will is our will? Yes! God, as individualized in you and me, exercises free will. God chooses self-expression through you and me as we were created to be.

When you choose God, that is your God Self, you move forward from that point as per your specific design. You will be attracted to and choose to move into your areas of specialization. Are you a mover and a shaker? Are you a healer or teacher? Are you a wanderer or creator? Are you an explorer or gardener? Who are you? What are you designed for and want to do? What does your heart say? Be true to you and you will live in the heart of your truth. You determine who you are now that you've accomplished your healing journey.

This is where the creative part of you becomes animated. This is where that Self you've been working to rescue is set loose and begins to actively explore. This is where you, on your heroic journey, begin to uncover and express your path of service.

There are only a few such paths ultimately, but they do come in many fascinating variations. We are spoiled with choice. Behind the curtain of our defenses we had no choice. We were stagnant and focused on survival.

Now, we have true choice, and abundantly so. We have choice beyond our wildest expectations.

When writers and artists come to this point in their journey they refer to this emerging referent as connecting with that "still small voice" within. Such voices are hard to hear amid the cacophony of busy and chaotic existences. Now we can hear this voice because we are out from under the tyranny of our defenses. This voice can be heard and felt, by tuning into it, learning to listen for its subtle nuances as these can be distinguished from our ordinary inner chatter. This is the undercurrent to our conscious outer directed lives. We will have greater insights, more creative thoughts and more intuitive glimpses about who we are and what direction to pursue. These may feel strange at first, but oddly personal. We will know they are meant exclusively for us.

Some of us will hear this voice loud and clear, and create great works of art and engineering as a result. Others will receive subtler messages, but pressing all the same, and these will lead them on their path of Conscious Evolution. By choosing to listen to ourselves, we will act appropriately for who we are and why we came to participate in this unfolding drama.

Heaven has no other purpose for us than to see us recreate it right here on Earth. Not the heaven of our illusions and childhood dreams, but a transcendence that sees people maximize their potential in an ever expanding interrelationship with each other. The old glue of love will bind us together once again. We will be well informed and well served by listening closely to each other. We will receive messages from each other and know they are valid because they reverberate with our hearts. This will be God talking to God and listening to God, as us. How can we fail?

We will know what is accurate for us because our still small voice will ratify incoming data as exclusively ours. We will move forward in the new direction. Trusting the voice, our inner pulse, and all of its possible configurations will allow this to happen. Remember, we are no longer circumscribed by our old defenses. We can move forward now and trust the information we are receiving is truly ours. It is hard, if not impossible, to fool a person who is well grounded in their own reality and in touch with their essential Self. This particular aspect of our heartfelt experience is what makes the whole process of moving forward so stable.

God had this in mind originally, not the unanticipated wide detour we took as individuals and a collective, this side journey which distracted us from our ultimate purpose. What we needed, once we took ourselves off the main path, lay dormant within each of us. It was emissaries of God, the "keepers of the truth," enlightened women and men across the centuries that helped to awaken us and lead us back on track. Now we are at this new threshold, contemplating our next horizon, ready to fully engage this emerging structure called the Self. This central driving force is what connects us directly to God, the Creator, and takes us forward on our new adventure. That is mythology in action.

Here we are now, consciously advancing the Creator's causes as has always been the plan. We are back on track. Where do we go from here?

The heroic journey inevitably leads to a path of service based on the unique traumas and challenges one has faced and overcome. If that is a path of healing, then helping others heal is what it will be. If that is a path of teaching, then teaching others will be the mainstay at this juncture. All heroes and heroines pass through their own trials first. They must overcome their demons, losses and heartaches before instructing others on how to do the same. We, who are moving forward now, have inscribed these tenets in our healing journey. We have taken up the reigns of helping others once our own healing had moved along. We are prepared to teach the upcoming generation those skills which have been so hard won. We must pass on what we have learned. That's how we, as individuals, serve the wider collective of mankind.

As the healers among us propagate their truth and assist others in their own unfolding, then more healers will be available to fill the gaps left by those who are moving forward. When any potential healer has finished grieving, she or he is ready to enter the fold and choose a path of service. We cannot heal others while we are in mourning. We can only heal ourselves at that point. But once that work is completed, we can become a helper and healer if that's where our next horizon points. It is only at this juncture that our path of service comes into view.

Then together, all of us, healers and teachers, will march in unison and inform the next group, those still lost in grief, what is involved in overcoming their suffering and what they need to move beyond. At some point we will leave these tasks to the next graduating group of healers and teachers, and we will become teachers of a different sort. We pass on what we have learned, and share every nuance with those coming behind us. The great cycle of life is at work once again.

All healers have been in the throes of grief at one time in their lives. Many chose to become healers as a result of their experiences. We will step into and out of such roles several times before we are done with them. Then we seek a new order of being to take us to our central purpose of learning. Growing and learning is what we are here to do. Growing is what God wants for us. This opportunity is available to everyone. Our existences are marked by these precepts, and we live and breathe them with each day of our presence on this planet.

We will review this in our next chapter. For now, suffice it to say that the new threshold is upon us. We are geared up and poised to take it on. Our healing journey has given us the tools to take the next step. Our particular brand of healing has prepared us for our purpose. Once healed, we can activate that purpose. That is what we are here to do.

Paying Attention

Attention! Attention! Attention! This is what is wrong with this place. We don't always pay close attention to our external circumstances. Yes, we now know, the inner life is vastly more real. But it is also true that the outer life informs that reality. We look in mirrors when we look out there. There is no compromise on this point. One informs the other.

When you get up in the morning do you dress yourself with eyes closed? Of course not! You look at what you're doing. You choose colors according to your mood and your personal sense of style. You look forward to the day and prepare to present yourself in the best possible light. Plaids do not go with polka dots.

So how is it that we continue to forget and choose to block out certain experiences? Are we not blinding ourselves to some essential reality? Of course we are. This is a survival mechanism. We've been doing it since the dawn of time. Children do it all the time. Blocking out unpleasantness is a common strategy until we realize we are re-creating and meeting the same issue and situation over and over again.

These unmet challenges recycle. As an adult, you are responsible for your life and for handling these issues as they are presented. In adulthood you come to believe that you can take care of yourself. But what do you do if you feel you can't? Do you rely on others? They have their lessons too. What we learn to do is work at this together.

We share with each other what we can. The rest we set aside for another day when we are better able to handle the bigger challenges. For now, we concentrate on what's in front of us. And the key to getting there is: Attention!

10 – The Road to Discovery

In every epoch in history there are seekers and discoverers. Those who have been forging their way up to the present are on the brink of new discoveries. They have overcome great obstacles to get where they are, and the treasure awaiting them is what all explorers seek, the truth of their Soul waiting to be released.

In days of old, these truths were passed on in secret ceremonies. Heroes and heroines were sent on a journey to discover their true Self by confronting a series of challenges that were put before them. Today's heroes and heroines are no different. Their new found Selves are the result of circumstances they have faced and overcome. Now they are ready to move ahead into the next cycle, that of teaching what they have gained experientially. It is here that their radical shift takes place. They must become teachers to pass on the newly gained knowledge.

A healer is no longer a healer when the last of her wounds has been cleansed and healed. Now, the healer becomes a teacher, a teacher of the truth of lessons learned. Seekers coming forth and approaching that particular threshold will find comfort in the knowledge that they, too, can win this battle. Healing journeys do have an end, and one's sights can be set beyond. It is here where transitions take place, on the cusp of ending one episode while the next adventure rises over the horizon.

This helps the explorer move from random searching to the realm of Conscious Evolution. Choosing discovery means we have arrived. We are at the Promised Land and the Golden Fleece is at hand, as are all the great prizes cited in so many historical accounts, especially the prize of the Soul. Our Souls, we come to understand, has many such journeys to take, and this is but one of them.

Each achievement for the Soul sets the tone for a pattern that repeats itself with regularity. This pattern cannot be discerned until the seeker arrives at the doorstep of full discovery and rescue of the Soul. Only from this vantage point can the whole panorama of what has transpired be viewed. All the subtle nuances that served as gentle reminders earlier are now present in bold relief, clearly delineated from their fuzzy origins. The seeker can literally see what they've been through in his or her march toward the Soul and why it had to proceed in a particular fashion.

It is here that the hero or heroine recognizes the order and value in all that has transpired in their lives. They can now see that every detail of their life has meaning. Nothing has been wasted. Everything has a purpose in helping them reach the next threshold. Their whole existence, this time around, was predicated on the insistence that at the Soul level, this is the way it had to be. To move from where they were to where they are now, they had to travel a particular road of trials. By doing so, they realize the road's function in their lives.

This is quite an arresting experience. Suddenly, everything makes sense. The Divine entering our lives, the mysteries that drove us to seek help, the pain we endured along the way and the players we came across were all part of the journey. This is when God speaks directly to us in our hearts and assures us with words that instill confidence within; "I knew you could do it. And you thought it wasn't possible."

Oh yes, God is speaking to us now, loudly and clearly. Amid the cacophony of our previous lives we couldn't hear "The Voice." But at this juncture, it is unmistakable. The Divine is at the helm and we know it in our hearts. Only our egos have a bad time accepting this realization. The ego wants desperately to be in charge. And history has presented us with many examples of where egos can take nations to war, to conquest, and yes, even to mass suicide. Egos do not have the capacity to lead, only to conquer and accumulate. For the ego is always in competition with other egos and sees the world as "us versus them." The Self knows we are all joined and leads from the heart. Cooperation, compassion and empathy are the order of the day.

What the ego tries to achieve is a travesty and a trick of mirrors, so to speak. Our egos thought they were in charge only to discover the pedals they were pushing were actually disconnected from any real mechanism. Someone or something else, in a clearly different part of the vehicle (our body/mind/spirit), was at the helm. This proves to be a bad day for the ego. That is clearly part of the journey, to dethrone that petty despot who desperately wants to be in control. The ego further discovers, I might add, that its need for control actually ran the vehicle into the ditch, repeatedly.

Time and time again, seekers of every stripe have made that sorry discovery, and to their dismay. "What was I thinking?" they might ask as they wake up to this fact. We will all ask that at least once in our lives, but more than likely many times over. Nevertheless, we made it to this next threshold, didn't we? Here we are, poised on that new brink, ready to carry our new discoveries and achievements forward.

This takes us back to where we started, we realize, as now we are armed with the truth. We have arrived in the land of right-mindedness. We no longer celebrate the stupidity that the ego clung to. We are on this threshold of an emerging vitality, rising to meet the Divine through our own inner awareness, to glorify the truth and sing praises to our own divinity in the process. At some level, we knew we could, once we committed to that wondrous vision before us. The Divine stands waiting, arms open wide, ready to receive all prodigals, as each of us returns from the frontiers of an ego-centered position to the discovery of our Heart and Soul. Tired and beleaguered as many of us are, we remain eager. We are ready to claim the Divine as our true heritage and release the folly that took us far and wide on that journey through time.

So many wonderful memories now align in such a fashion as to provide a linear view of what has just happened. The seeker's life lies stretched out with each point on the line representing some crucial turning point on their quest. No wonder they feel tired at this juncture. They've traveled such a wide and varied road. How could they maintain that energy and pace? That's what we all wonder when we undertake our own review, looking over our shoulder at what just transpired, standing at this new juncture with discovery in our hands.

This is an amazing place to be. Many great artists have passed here before us and illustrated this point in their work. Thomas Merton, Michelangelo, William Shakespeare and Albert Einstein are good examples. "The Lord is thy Shepherd, thou shall not want" is the truth that all the greats have claimed before us. And even moderns like John Lennon illustrated this kind of knowing in his great song "Imagine." So many great movers and shakers, past and present have charted the path we've just come through. Yes indeed, they were there before us. But so are we now, and we are the new generation of Lightworkers ready to take the world forward into its next stage of evolution.

Are you ready? A few of us may not yet be. But many more will deliver a resounding "Yes" rising from their throats and leaping from Soul to Soul, reverberating and resonating around the world, inspiring all that are ready to take that next step forward. This is part of the journey, the activation of the lights of those ready to move forward, but waiting and wanting someone to show them the way.

This is the task of the new discoverers; those of you who have journeyed down that path of healing and are now ready to teach. This is the purpose you've been waiting to identify, actualize and begin to deliver. It's time to teach what you know. What better way can there be to move you forward once again? A teacher gets to integrate all that has been learned, to be comfortable and at home with it, before the next challenge is presented. Teaching is simply the best way to move forward on one's journey past healing. We do for others what has been done for us, what we have accomplished for ourselves, what we are ready to practice without embarrassment or shame. Yes, we are ready!

This is where God needs us now, and we are conscious of that need. The Voice of God speaks to us directly from our hearts. We are encouraged and directed to listen and to listen intently. The Voice will become clearer with time and practice. We know this to be true because we feel this Spirit permeate every fiber of our being once we are fully attuned to it.

This is the truth that we've been seeking, the truth that's been lurking in the shadows. All those subtle hints that we took note of before are clearly perceptible now. That was God's Voice all along. We couldn't quite make it out. Now there is no mistaking it. The great artists told us about that "still small voice." The great psychologists and social scientists of our time have been repeating the very same message.

This information is historical and factual, as well as currently valid. The "still small voice" exists, and it lives within every one of us, but not so quiet anymore. Our discovery has been made. We have arrived. Every myth in history speaks of this moment. It is cataclysmic. It has never happened before in our lifetime, but it is here now.

"Oh ecstasy," we often say in the midst of great moments. We are simply awestruck. We are at an epiphany of existence, one with God, one with ourselves, wholly integrated, alive and free. No more dogmas! No more lies! No more fears! No more doubts! God leads the way and we know it in our hearts. We are finally out of the desert. How wonderful this feels.

As we move on from here, we do so with grace and finesse, with a confidence unparalleled to this point in our lives. We are senior students in a world filled with juniors scrambling to find their way. "If only they could see what I see," we wonder impatiently. But they will, we realize, as soon as someone steps in to help them along. That is our job now, to bring the message to all who are still seeking and working their way through self-discovery. This will be the very world we have just uncovered and claimed, and are now ready to set about mapping.

This is the other purpose behind the process of discovery. It must be followed by teaching. The new world needs to be uncovered, mapped and described. There are other worlds still waiting beyond, but this one has to be understood first. Systems of uncovering and proper elucidation can be applied to each new territory as these methods have been applied in previous endeavors. What needs to be learned has begun. The New World is born. Let us bring it to life!

You Are Enough

What is it that prompts us to try and appear grander than we are? Is it to save face, or some other non-important goal that drives us to this? Are the contortions required to change oneself, and quite dramatically at times, really worth it? Is it not sad that, while having been blessed with such a humble and yet glorious beginning, we then go out and change it to something less, just to please others?

Would God change into something to impress others? Highly unlikely! So why do we do it? God is already impressed with who we are. After all, we are God's creation.

God says to us, "Know this, and know this for certain – You are enough!" It is unnecessary to change what you are for another's sake. There is no legitimate reason to do so. For those who feel they are not enough, God wants us to get to know our true Self, our inner core, our complete being, and to learn how great we already are. Most of us have only caught a glimpse of our totality. There remains much to be uncovered.

Let's explore then, shall we? Let's discover who we really are, from the inside out, and show this to the world. We will all be impressed by this discovery and learn from it. Then we will all know for certain: "I, We, You - are enough!"

11 – The Circle

It seems uncanny that those who make the discoveries and then map out the new territory are themselves wounded heroes and heroines rising from their challenges and moving out into the world to share what they have gained. They have much to teach us. They are the army of groundbreakers who have undertaken to bring forth the lessons of their hard-won journeys. But how are the rest of us going to prepare for what's ahead if we don't have these early adventurers to take us along and prepare us for our challenges ahead?

Only scouts, in previous times, were trusted with such tasks as they were experienced in uncovering upcoming hazards and reporting these to the column following behind. Winding their way through mountain passes, surrounded by unseen and unheard dangers, they would lie motionless for hours waiting to see when it was safe to move forward again. These scouts were the radicals, like-minded in some ways, and always ahead of the mainstream. Their pleasure came in discovering the new and sharing that with the group following behind. The leaders of each column waited to hear those reports before ushering their charges along. These leaders were the wise ones who took heed of the information and, in consultation with the scouts, translated it into terms the rest of the group could understand.

Scouts and group leaders had a unique purpose which ultimately made a beneficial contribution to the whole. The waiting column of settlers relied on the leaders to guide them to the Promised Land. These weary travelers relied on scouts and leaders to pave the way. They waited to be told what was to happen next. And they followed, sometimes grumbling, but followed nevertheless.

Today's generation of seekers and travelers are in for a big surprise. No longer can they just rely upon the knowledge provided by scouts and leaders who interpreted incoming information and made unilateral decisions on how to proceed. This time the image of a growing community and its individuals is a circle, and in a circle everyone shares what they know to enrich the whole.

The concept of the circle has deep historical roots, well before Christianity. The circle was the manner in which so-called primitive groups shared information with each other on an egalitarian basis. There were no leaders per se, only shareholders who assisted in interpreting the tapestry of events and information confronting the group.

The circle as a whole represents that unity that we are now seeking. We became lost when we allowed the column metaphor to dominate our thinking. That was the hierarchical system which implied only a select few "knew," and the rest had to follow on faith. This is no longer acceptable. Each of us has to resume the positions we once held as equal and responsible members of the whole. Individuals must now gather in a circle and share what they know. This makes a group larger and stronger than in a column made up of the same number of members. It is a collaborative structure based on the premise that each of us has a unique gift to offer the whole. This is the case in all walks of life, especially the circles of old.

Today's small-groups movement is an example of the return to the sharing circle, something North America's aboriginal peoples clearly understood. Based on the premise of true equality and sharing for the common good, this emerging recognition of what was once common is a return to the old. For how can we help each other if we are pre-empted in our efforts to share what we know? We no longer need a hierarchical system. We need our individual connection to the Divine.

Soon, we will all be able to hear that "still small voice" speaking to us from within. And it is this very ability coupled with our unique understanding that will allow us to share as equals. We will be speaking from the same vantage point, with God as our influence, instructing us on how to conduct ourselves in the present and future.

The power mongers of the world are currently not pleased with this eventuality, as their privileged positions are already being called into question. They will have to descend into the "ranks" and become one of us - no better and no worse - just another member of the group sharing what they know. It will be a difficult time for them as it will be for all of us crossing that threshold into the Eternal. God waiting there, embracing each of us as we scramble over the parapet to find ourselves in the Holy Land of our own Souls!

This will be difficult at first, but after a time it will become a routine part of the curriculum, taught in schools and community gathering places all around the world. The message will be heard by each one of us and provide direction as to how we are to conduct ourselves as part of a circle. At that point we will have grown up. We will have transformed ourselves into a legion of emissaries, here to do God's work in the most efficient manner. Then we will begin to design and build those vehicles required to take humanity into the wilds of the Universe, to learn about the great mysteries that exist there, to understand and describe what they are, and then to move on to the next mystery after that.

Such an effort cannot be accomplished by a group of bedraggled stragglers marching solemnly in a single column. We must work in unison for this great leap to take place. Only in doing so, can this leap of faith into the heart of this new millennium, with all of its promises, can actually be accomplished.

We are here on this threshold, friends. This is where we are now and to what we are pointing just ahead. Our next step awaits us. Let us see what that brings.

Friendship

Sometimes when we are feeling lost and alone, we don't know which way to turn to renew a friendship. That close friend we had so long ago seems lost to us now. They have faded away like so many things from our earlier life.

Are we to believe that we can no longer sustain such relationships? Are we to let go of all those sources of comfort that once enjoined us and caused us great pride?

Our affections for others are what keep us alive. Our connections to each other invite us to live again, to breathe in, and to satisfy those cravings for friendship we once carried and then set aside for what appeared to be more important matters.

It is untrue that we have to let go of such connections as time marches on. What is in fact true is that we have a greater need for each other as the years speed on by.

When we feel alone, then we are alone, but not in the literal sense. And when we are together it is because we feel connected. Connected means enjoined. It means we are happy to work together with one common goal. The Source of our being brings us constant comfort.

Now we are ready to move on, to rejoin with each other and share what we have learned to cherish on life's journey. The twilight of life is far more comfortable when our lessons have taught us about the value and importance of good companions during this pilgrimage Home.

Home is where the heart is, and that is where we all come together in the end.

12 – The Voice

When the Creator's voice universally announces Itself from within, we will have arrived at the dawning the next Golden Era for the human race. This is the vanguard of the new era, one in which all members of the humanity will be duly informed from within.

Like our fictional characters in *The Voice – A Mythological Guide to Mankind's Ascension*, we will be alerted to our duty by our direct line to Source. This Voice will announce Itself as our Higher Self and begin instructing us on the ways of the world and how to handle our lives more efficiently. No longer will we be guided by some external authority's interpretations of what's best for us. No longer will we be limited in our thinking by the charismatic enticements of would be soothsayers, pretend religious leaders or pseudo authority figures of any type. In times of old and to our present day, such individuals were the status quo, the ones we gave our power to, because we were sold on the idea that they knew better. Their days are now done.

In modern parlance, we might refer to the director within as the ego, that puppet of domination who presumes to know what's best for us, as long as we are willing to let it have its way. Having moved through recovery we know in our hearts that this portion of the personality is no longer valid as a leader. Removing the ego from its dominant post will lay to rest our need for external control and manipulation. The circle becomes a possibility now because we do not need a programmed ego to be in control or to be controlled by others. Puppet dictators fall to the wayside, along with egos and other pretenders to the throne of our thinking. They are destined for the garbage heap, no longer necessary, no longer desired, as soon as we choose to govern ourselves.

These artifacts of old are finished as we move into this new century and millennium. We need a new standard, a new vision for our purpose and efforts, a new concept of how to proceed and unfold our talent and true worth. The Voice speaks loudly now as we learn to listen effectively. We see and hear for ourselves what God needs, wants, and orchestrates for our unfolding. Each new vision and not so subtle hint leads us into the mind of God and shows us God's purpose. We always have the privilege of refusing, as has always been the case with free will, but as the drama unfolds and we see the ultimate picture come into clearer focus, it will be increasingly difficult to step away from the promise of what wonders lie before us.

We will be shown only what is in our hearts and, therefore, what we would desire to accomplish for our spectacular unfolding. God is a presence, not an oligarchy. This presence is something we sense, an inner stirring and emerging direction that engages our heart and moves us forward on our truest path. "Follow your bliss," is how Joseph Campbell summarized this call to personal authority.

God's path for us is our path for ourselves. We are informed of God's will, yet we remain free to choose. We are free to be as happy as we can. Letting go of struggle, we can choose that which suits us best. It is easy, after all, being God ourselves, to choose one's truest path when one hears the voice of reason from within our heart.

God asks us to commit to "thy will." In so doing we are honoring ourselves since we are intractably one with God. We are together again and comforted by the knowledge that we are indeed One. So making decisions is no longer an uncertain matter. We know of what we speak because we feel it in our hearts. And we know of what God speaks because we feel that in our hearts as well. We cannot fail with this awareness.

To repeat--failure is simply not possible. When we are finally linked to the truth and can hear and feel it clearly for ourselves, we can only make the best of choices. But to do this, we must know our hearts to the depths of our being. How do we get there? Where does this part of the journey begin?

We see in The *Voice*, that the characters are unfolding by attending to their internal referents. These referents are called feelings in modern parlance, feelings which ascertain the state of our being from moment to moment. Listening to our feelings, we quickly realize, is no small task. It requires trust and faith in us, something we have been conditioned away from by the various authority figures in our lives, especially organized religion. Not surprisingly, we do not immediately achieve that level of faith on our own. Because the authority figures in our lives taught us not to trust ourselves, we need help to reacquire what was originally a natural gift and skill.

It seems contradictory that the very nature of our being is what we've been conditioned away from by authorities who claimed to know what our faith should be about. The sign of the times is the dysfunctional family which begins at home and extends into our religious family with its convoluted scripts, contradictory interaction patterns and double-binds that create untenable psychological conflicts. This is who we are today and what we are trying to evolve from. It is through trusting our feelings that we eventually break the cycle of guilt and shame that are always followed by self-abuse. The patterns of neurosis and self-defeating behavior we see today constitute our heritage from this dysfunctional family influence, including the major religions of our times.

We can trace this rupture in our healthy evolutionary process directly to institutionalized religion. At their insistence, we began distancing ourselves from our natural Self. Some theories suggest that we, as a species, wanted to move away from our center, to experience something different so we could return more enlightened than when we set out. It really doesn't matter if this is true. How we came to abandon our Self is not as important anymore as how we regain that natural state. This is the plight of many modern day seekers and defines the psychology of our times. We became lost in the morass of dysfunctional living perpetrated by the political and religious institutions of the time. We were taught, implicitly and explicitly, to lie to ourselves and hence to each other, to avoid the pain within. In so doing, we actually created more pain for ourselves. We were then taught by our religious overseers that we needed more faith, their brand of faith, to deal with the suffering their poisonous system was subtly delivering. We came to believe these lessons and foisted them on ourselves and our children. The trap had been set and sprung, with us in it. We've been scratching our heads ever since. We tried to make sense of what happened, but used outdated and perverse paradigms to do so. That's how we became enslaved to religion.

This is a sad state we find ourselves in. Lying to ourselves, and then looking outside ourselves for some type of salvation. We re-capture the flavor of this rift in the reliability of the hero myth. The hero is required to travel to the underworld to rescue a child that's chained to a wall. The child is being watched by a guard dog. This is Cerberus in myth, or negative ego as a contemporary reference. The hero does not attack the dog, but wins the dog's trust before rescuing the child from its chains. Heroes meet a host of characters during this process, including images of authority figures that have to be addressed. The hero is always assisted by a God or Goddess figure in their venture who helps them find their way. The story ends when the hero and heroine have their prize, the rescued child as metaphor for their reclaimed true Self.

The goal of depth therapy is to uncover and reconnect with the Self. The Self is our direct connection to the Soul. The Soul is where the heart is. The heart is our feeling center and where our Soul resides. The Soul is the Voice of God within each of us. We are all on a journey toward reclaiming God as ourselves, and that journey leads straight to the heart of our being. It is here we must retrieve those abandoned parts of ourselves, left behind as a result of our dysfunctional influences, and clamoring for attention ever since.

Our therapy takes us back to center and teaches us to accept and then trust ourselves again. Now begins a new journey, a journey of awakening and working directly with God. A new metaphor is required. The hero's journey is behind us. What lies ahead?

The image of the circle is where we are led to now as collaboration becomes the new necessity. We continue to deal with our selves. We have arrived at a new level of maturity. What now? We know the old rules no longer apply. And we can't turn to our ego/protector because it has been properly demoted and placed back where it belongs, in a role secondary to that of the heart.

What we are facing now is a new world, where the rules are not yet known, where the motives seem difficult to find, where the features of the landscape are veiled in unfamiliarity. We are in the New World, the place where heroes arrive after their self-rescuing quest. Now we have work to do. We must define who we are using a new set of parameters. We must meter out knowledge as we acquire it. We must announce to the world the truth of our arrival and the validity of our heroic undertaking.

Too many of the hero and heroine's contemporaries will continue to cycle through dysfunctional dilemmas rather than take a chance on the New World. They are comfortable with the land of recovery and afraid to leave it behind in order to grow beyond. But they will be watching and they will take note of those heroic individuals who will live life guided by their new found center of being. Eventually those watching will cross over, realizing that this is a worthy step and take on this new way of being. They will learn many new things too. The New World has a new set of rules and we will be required to learn them if we wish to proceed.

The first of these new rules is that there are no rules, unlike the era of ego domination. The second is that heroes and heroines do not conquer anymore - they listen! They pay attention to what's going on inside and listen to their cohorts whom they have come to realize are equally heroic. Thirdly, they operate from a base called Love. Not the love depicted in romantic or sexual relationships, but Love as a living breathing entity, as the very essence of our being, our place in the world, and our connection with the Divine.

We will know where we belong and that we have a right to be wherever we wish. That right was divinely granted and is immediately accessible through our inner referents. In our feeling center we know the truth because we battled our way to this truth, and left no stone unturned in the process. This is hard-won privilege, no longer to be relinquished at any external entity's behest, and no longer to be doubted by ourselves. What is unveiled here is the truth, as if God were standing there showing it to us.

There will be no denial and questioning either. We will know it to be the truth. Those who cannot accept this are those who still live in the 3rd dimension of consciousness dominated by ego and fear. These people are not quite ready for this brand of truth. When they do arrive, and they will, they too will seize it and never let go. Never! Once you attain that level of understanding, you know for certain you are standing on solid and divinely imbued ground!

So the tools of this New World are plenty. Some of the new tools may look like those older tools. You know what these new tools can do for you and you see that they behave in a vastly different fashion. In an oligarchy, tribute was paid to a singular individual, or some elite group, which stood outside and above individual citizens, and delivered proclamations. In the circle of Love, there are no such individuals. Now attention is paid to the inner voices of the Self and with the inner truth of the heart.

In the book, *The Voice*, our students on Planet Rapture did exactly that, they learned to listen to the Self and began to uncover those final layers of defense and denial before The Voice came through loud and clear. They heard the same universal messages, but they also received personal messages tailored to their specific lives. They received direct instruction from their God Self. The enigma for them, and for us, is that these connections were available all along, but out of reach while so-called external experts and egos held sway.

Here we have a preview of what's ahead. Our characters from *The Voice* learned to survive and flourish with those new tools such as truth, inner assurance, self-acceptance, self-responsibility and love. They heard the Voice, and accepted the challenge of practicing the new ways. We, too, shall learn such things as we move along. Our lessons have already begun. The stage is set. We have engaged the new curriculum. We help it unfold as we step forward. What an amazing experience this will be. Discover the new path and teach the new path! Let's see what happens next.

Companions

What are we to make of our adventures when God steps in to help us along? "A friend in need is a friend indeed." When we are alone we can imagine all kinds of disasters and frighten ourselves into paralysis. This is of no value to anyone. Unable to move, we may never strike out to discover what could be ours.

The Universe holds numerous opportunities that can help us break from our conventional mold. Companions come and go. They each bring something to the relationship, a bit of whimsy, a bowl of flowers, a simple gesture of approval, a kind word. Each such act and person demonstrates that we are not alone and that there's plenty of support for all.

So why do we insist that we have to do it alone? It's not possible. No one gets through life alone. We are certainly well influenced by each other and supported in some measure. "Bring two or three together," God says, "and watch them unfold graciously. Bring Me one who feels they are alone and I will show you a sad and lonely heart."

We weren't designed to be alone. Having companions is part of our purpose. All of our senses work toward that same goal. When we work together, we help each other. When we are alone, we pine for another to join us. It is only together that we can share what we are investigating and learning.

Being alone is good for incubation. Coming together is where we get to show what it is we dreamed. Sometimes such dreams manifest to include and affect everybody regardless of how personal it appeared in the beginning. Such is the story of mankind's major achievements and so many great works of art. All are rewarded by each other's creations.

Share your stories and life experiences. You have something to say, just as we all do. We will all benefit from each other's contributions. Reach into your heart and share yours today.

13 – A New World

An oligarchy falls. A new truth arises. Where do we go from here? It is the task of all heroes to first discover the new land and then to tame it. This requires stealth and determination, to boldly go where most fear to tread. Initially, heroes and heroines go it alone. They report back what they find. They instruct and they teach. They tantalize with tales of the new, the unknown, the yet to be discovered and what will soon be appreciated by all. Eventually we all arrive. We arrive at our own time and our own pace. That will be soon enough.

In the meantime, the heroes and heroines who have arrived are busy. They have to map out this new territory, give it a name, learn its ways and deliver those findings to the ones quickly coming up. Those who are more learned must hurry to make good their assessments and set up the structures to teach what they have learned. The movement is afoot and cannot be denied.

In this case, there is an unusual dilemma within the whole process. Heroes of the present have discovered that true empowerment comes from within. No one can teach this to another unless that individual is prepared to receive. There will be many who immediately declare that they are ready. There will be those who will refuse, insisting that our heroes perhaps just tell them what to do. In this case our heroines will be faced with another dilemma as a feature of the new territory. They will be faced with resistant ones who simply want to hang on to the old ways and be led into the new territory. The lack of self-responsibility that allowed them to give over their power to external authorities will still be at play. Out of ignorance or fear, they may turn their backs on this opportunity.

Instead, many resistant ones will try to shame our heroes into returning to the old ways. This will be a test. Pangs of loneliness will run through them. But the pull of the new will be too strong to resist, and honoring the Self will be impossible to ignore. Growth always seeks growth and heroes are in pursuit of that end.

Resistant ones, along with our disenfranchised egos, will be left behind. Those that resist change, even when it's for the better, will be buried in the sands of time along with the many remnants of similar civilizations that stayed stuck in their ways. Whether outward, or inward, when civilizations refuse to grow, only their monoliths remain and stand quiet and withering in the desert winds. Their messages to us and what they've learned are no longer available. Sadly, it is the passing of an era, but a necessary one. The stories of Atlantis and Lemuria come to mind at this point. So many thousands of years later we have uncovered mere fragments of what they had achieved and still wonder what they had to offer.

For those of us standing at the vanguard of this new era, it will be a sad time as well. We may be leaving behind so many familiar faces that were part of our journey. We must leave them behind as the new territory opens up. Ours is a new task and we must forge on to keep growing and feel alive. You see, our heroic adventure is our life. Without this pull, this force, this inner stirring, we would feel ourselves dry up and wither away, just like those stone monoliths in the deserts of past civilizations. We must press on, to not only survive, but to thrive. That is the nature of our growth.

Press on we do, heroes and heroines of this new age. We move forward now, with or without our favored friends and family. We move on because that is what our hearts beg us to do. "Come along now," the heart beckons, "I need you; come along and help me open up the new world." And we will respond with eager acquiescence. We know we must do this for ourselves and for our Higher Self who is now our guiding beacon.

Echoes of the past still linger. The voices of old reassert themselves from time to time, especially when we take another step forward. But these voices are no longer formidable foes. They've lost their power to sway. We learned much about displacing our critical voices and we know in our hearts who speaks the truth. These negative judgmental voices are simply echoes of a dying era. What emerges in their place is a whole and new life.

Ahead we march, heroes and heroines, driven by that inner urge to strive and open new doors, to take chances and prepare the path for others. So many seekers will be coming soon and they will need guidance to make their way. Not everyone will be informed by their Souls at this time. So those of us who are connected will show the way. But what we are leading them to is their Selves, not ours. To always be moving toward that one true source that lies at the center of everyone's being is the main goal for all. This connection is available for all who are ready to receive.

We, as heroes and heroines of our age, will know that the Divine broadcast is on all the time. We will have sharpened our facility to tune in at will. We will have opened that final door permanently and will never go back. Those friends who call to us from our past will be sad to see us go. Their cries for our return have to be ignored. For those of us awakening at this time, the march is on. The Army of Light is coming together and it is ready to move forward again!

We say again, because this process has happened before in our human history. There have been other times where general awakenings have occurred. These have been sporadic yet persistent all the same. Great cultures have come and gone, leaving us a few artifacts to mark their passing. Among these are evidences of their awakening processes. Some of these features were laid down in great books and passed on to future generations. Others, sadly, were lost in the winds that nip at the heels of passing cultures.

We learn from their remaining contributions. We carefully read their inscriptions, hoping to find some elements of truth to help us on our journey. Those artifacts do exist as pearls of wisdom scattered down through the ages. And they all say the same things:

"Pay attention to your Self!"

"Love your neighbor!"

"Listen to your heartbeat!"

"Know that God is within you!"

"Know that you are truth!"

"Know all of these things and set your Self free!"

"Find your way Home and I'll be glad to receive you!"

The words of the Divine echo throughout the pages of time. From one great book to another! From one great culture to another! The same invitation is always extended: "Find your way home and you will be set free." How can we fail? How can we go astray?

Going astray is something we seem to have done many times over centuries. But finding ourselves again seems equally plausible and quite achievable when reviewing the lives of our ancestors and cultures, past and present. We always seem to muddle through. Maybe it's because the Divine is there with us, heroes nudging us along, showing us the way.

Well, here we are again, back at this old and new territory. We are back at the place where monoliths were left and heroes forged ahead to map out a new direction to be followed. Here we are at the dawn of a new era, a threshold that beckons us forward with its promise of unlimited abundance, ecological beauty and personal wisdom. We are fortunate to be here, receiving these gifts. We are ready for this new venture. God urges forward, so onward we plod. We've come through the process of recovery. Where do we go next?

Heroes and heroines report back to the upcoming students. There's a new way ahead, one that all of us can follow, one that is a sure fire hit and will guide us to a wonderful destiny. The new truth is of this earth and spirit. It is beyond our ego and those simpler views of old. It comes from our depths and informs our lives. For years we've heard about that "still small voice" from within. Now, this Voice has become louder.

More and more people are hearing of The Voice. They are tuning in and receiving directly. All of our truths are there to be told. The Voice does not discriminate or mislead. All of us are being informed by God within, from the depths of our being. We are in touch with Soul and Soul listens only to God. Therefore, we are in direct contact with God:

"Welcome to my Home. My Home is your Home and yours is also mine. We are in this together. I will be contacting you regularly now. Please listen to your feelings and pay attention to other signs. I have many ways of reaching you, each way being unique to you."

We listen to the advisements coming from our heroes and heroines as they forge ahead. We know they are fully aware of what they speak, and they speak only the truth. They have been telling us to listen for ourselves. Do not listen to their voices, listen to your own. The message is repeated until we all finally hear it.

"Listen to your heartbeat and your feelings! Know that I am there within you and among you. I am your source and liberator if that's what you need. Most assuredly, I am your Friend!"

This Voice will be heard by more and more of us each day. It will be abundantly clear that all are informed by that Voice and it will direct each and every one of us from this point onward.

This will be the voice of reason. It will be the voice of love. It will sound just like you. It will sound like God is speaking to you through an intercom on some occasions. This voice will be loud and clear, and distinctly your own. It will present you with messages that will not be accessible by anyone else. At other times, there will be general broadcasts where everyone is informed about the same events. This is what our characters in *The Voice* learn at the end.

God loves us all, we realize, and that's a great thing indeed. It is time we become aware of the process and start receiving for ourselves. The Divine speaks to each and every one of us in the very same fashion.

We can all hear that voice once we choose to awaken. We can all contact that place within where innocence resides and teaches us to be new again. We can all entertain this possibility. It is a choice. The heroes and heroines of the past have shown us how to proceed and find our way. Heroes and heroines of today are doing the same thing, revisiting the old mythology and attuning it to our times. This alerts us to our current purposes.

Listen! Yes, listen! The Voice of God is within you. Pay attention and you too will be informed of your life and purpose. You cannot be denied. Only through your denial can you be left behind. You will never be abandoned.

Here is another look into our future. We go now into the new land, where the new guidelines apply, those we have been addressing in this book. Listen closely and these will teach you about you. They will also teach you how to easily have your needs met, and how to express those gifts which were delivered from God to you. With your heart as guide and the eternal broadcast readily available, you are on your way.

Touch

What is it about touch that delivers us to Love? We know when we're being softly touched that it indeed feels good. A warm caress, a gentle stroke, they serve to awaken us to that Divine presence. It is this Divine presence which inhabits us all and to which we are awakening.

We used to believe that we were different from the Divine. Knowing now that our lives are interconnected, with the Divine and with each other, we begin to open ourselves to receiving without question or justification. To be touched by another not only feels good, but unlocks the door to feelings of worthiness within our inner Self.

When did we come to that juncture in our lives where we stopped receiving, as if to say "I don't really need that anymore?" We all need physical contact. We are visceral. We feel. We respond to a welcome touch with surrender. We recoil when blows are struck. We surrender when caresses make their way across our body.

It is sad to hear an adult say "I don't need that" when touch becomes unavailable. We are concerned with appearances here, not wanting to look needy. In receipt of touch we fear appearing weak, especially to ourselves.

In life there is no such person as one who needs nothing. There are, however, many who attempt to convince themselves that this is the case. When I need touching, I surrender. I receive. I extend my arms. I like it. It feels good. My children hug me and I hug them in return. This is so with my wife, our cat, dog and our friends. We all enjoy touching and encourage it. Real strength is to know what you need, ask for it and then prepare to receive.

Let yourself receive touch whenever it is offered, and be prepared to return the gesture with similar warmth. Get out there and hug somebody, appropriately of course, and let them hug you. Giving and receiving, that's what makes the world go round.

14 – Coming Home

Imagine going out into the wilderness on your own, with no desire except to notice what is going on around you. Can you see yourself doing that? Filling yourself with all those marvelous feelings, your senses coming alive and open, your heart leaping for joy at every sound and each discovery. Feel this magic in your heart as it unfolds through you. This is your life, magical and filled with Divine breath.

Life on Earth was designed to be an adventure from the first breath we took as we entered this world. It was meant to be exciting, titillating and challenging. I often wonder where I would be if I didn't know and believe this. The sweetness of life leaps into awareness. I take a deep breath and I am filled with nature's lore.

This is our task, to fill our cups and pursue all of what's available, and then instruct others on what we have learned. I know that this may sound radical, simplistic even, but that is not the case. It is the wonder of this world that counts. We are part of that wonder, and are to be counted among the flowers and the bees, the fruits in the trees and the great bounty that unfolds before us.

We are part of this pageantry as well, some of us blooming at different times than others. We are part of the harvest, one of the many crops that reflect back to the Divine another wondrous delight.

God's eyes are our eyes. The Divine sees through us and into this magical hinterland designed for our growth and evolution. We are set loose with a guiding light called consciousness, which absorbs and describes all of our adventures. We share our experiences, our thoughts and our feelings with those around us, and in so doing we maintain our connection with the Divine. This reciprocity and interconnectedness prepares us for more discoveries as we continue in our adventures.

Our hearts leap for joy with every discovery. Passion sets our hearts on fire. Passion moves us beyond measured boundaries. The gift of passion provides the impetus to leap over and beyond any perceived limitations, so we can discover a part of ourselves and the world that hitherto we were not aware.

There have been injunctions in our human history that advised us against taking such leaps before we are ready. Eating fruit from the Tree of Knowledge springs to mind as an example. There are times when we need to be cautious, but only because we are not ready for the next level of awareness such an experience would provide. It's no different than advising children that they are not ready for adolescent experiences or adolescents that they are not quite ready for adult experiences. It's a matter of maturation and preparedness that sets the stage for a successful leap forward.

What is essential, now, is that we see our readiness for the next threshold that is opening before us. It awaits our commitment to leap across. This is an invitation to progress by taking care of any challenges that may be blocking our view of the new realm. Whatever we are presented with is grist for the mill. Our growth will offer challenges that will also provide the tools to manage them.

Let's reflect again on where we began with the heroic journey and its concurrent growth process. The hero and heroine are learning the very lesson cited above, staying focused on what lies ahead, identifying the challenges, determining the necessary tools for mastery, and moving forward with renewed strength and agility. The Creator can't make it any more tantalizing than that, a tasty morsel of experience dangling before us. Who can say this is good or bad? Let's give it a try and find out. Every challenge is an invitation. Our Creator doesn't want us to stand still. The lessons from the Tree of Knowledge are over. We have discoveries to make and much learning to do. New options are being presented to us every day.

"Get out of your own way. Get moving again. It's time to march toward these new adventures. There may be perilous times ahead, but with your focus being on the Divinity that lies deep within you, you will be guided past troubling shoals. The days of misguided catechisms are gone. Some told you to stay put when the Divine needs you to move forward. Open your heart and your mind. You will be properly directed. Together, all of us who are divinely inspired, we will travel this adventure together. There is no need to fumble in the dark any longer. Now is the time to move forward with eyes and heart wide open."

We will hear this message in our hearts. We will know with certainty that such messages come to us through our Souls. Only our Souls can deliver the truth now. All those who would muzzle us are frightened. They are concerned that as we undertake to roam free, a freedom which at this time they do not comprehend, we will no longer defer to their 3rd dimensional world view. For them, this is a loss of power and control. They fear abandonment of all which, at this time of our impending ascension, has brought them the illusion of comfort and control.

We, who are growing, want more than worn out prescriptions at this stage in our development. We are hungry for truth, which is far more than trite clichés and worn out dogmas have to offer. Jesus said: "You shall do things greater than this," referring to the miracles for which he was credited. This statement may have once appeared as a simple metaphorical message to us from the past. But now it sounds out a trumpet call of greater possibilities, for each and every one of us on the ascension path.

Now is the time for us to return to these Divine lessons. The great cycle of life has come around to its beginning. This time we are at a new and unfamiliar doorstep. The message is age old, but now we are renewed. The time has come for us to step through and to see with our own eyes and hearts what truth lays waiting for us, within and without.

The adventure of self-discovery and the pursuit of the Divine within have brought us face to face with ourselves and with each other. The journey has been sometimes perilous, and occasionally there have been missteps along the way. But there were victories. All the challenges you were confronted with were designed to help you grow and mature, and to help you realize your true nature, the Divine nature of all.

Trajectory

Stranger things have happened, you say, than being found on this plane after years of stardust cleansing and comet chasing. It's a rare sight to see from that cosmic point of view. Out there everything seems possible and equally amazing. The gliding of planets, the circling of moons, stars streaking across the inky night, so much motion, so much animation, we can actually see it if we try.

How does that relate to what we do here? Nothing moves out there except in predictable patterns set in motion by the Creator of all that is. Could it be that we are that predictable as well? Do we actually have a direction that is our ideal? It would seem so!

We have a trajectory that is uniquely our own. It can be measured and anticipated if one knows the fundamentals of cosmic movements. All life forms move toward a higher order, a disassembly and reassembly at a new altitude. That is transformation. We become something more than we were, be it physically, psychologically and spiritually.

And what do we mean by more? The God likeness in us is that "more." We were brought into being by the Divine and we are being urged by this Force to move forward. It is right for us to expand, to gain knowledge and to grow. We do this as much for ourselves as we do it for all mankind. We do it to restore our individual Divinity and that of the collective. We want for ourselves that which we want for others and for this planet and the Universe. We have an unending appetite to grow.

We are powerless in that sense. We wish to express and actualize these desires. We are free to choose. We can always refuse, but that brings on the pain of separation. There are better choices to be had when we understand the dynamics of our own life. Our appetite for life propels us forward, not to merely survive, but to thrive. This is our Divine nature. To be at odds with it is to be odds with the basic laws of the Universe: all is ever-changing and ever-expanding. We are obliged to do both.

Profit yourself, now. Seek what is yours and ingest it fully. Grow! Expand! Flourish! Follow the bliss that is your path. And be kind to others as you move along. They are pursuing their path just like you and me. We are all part of a Divine team in training for the next big event. It is here now, and it is called Ascension.

Conscious Evolution

Part II

Ascension

15 – Once Upon a Time

"Now is the time for all good men to come to the aid of the party." That was a familiar phrase when I was learning to type, and leads me to the following story.

Once upon a time, there was a young man named Moe. He came into the world not knowing who he was or what his purpose here was to be.

Moe struggled all his life to "get, it" but he kept falling down again and again, as he had so many times before, because he wanted to know it all, and he could not. That brought him to this juncture in Life, trying to figure out who he is and what is his Life Purpose?

Our subject Moe, has been up and down this road many times, and still has to learn that he is okay being who he is. Who he is, in fact, is just perfect, thank you. He still has a lot to learn about that particular point.

Traveling on this journey through time, we try to learn who we are and look outside of ourselves for some form of measurement, usually attributed to our accomplishments and achievements.

If I were to say that you are a person of great authority, would you believe me--the person saying it to you--or you as the person denying it?.

Who defines us? "I do" should be your answer. But clearly that is not always the case.

For example, I define myself, in part, through my work. I also define myself through my accomplishments. And through my failures!

If I define myself by how others see me, I adopt an external viewpoint. I validate certain experiences as good and others as bad, poorly conceived or unacceptable, and so on. Again, I use that same external reference point to determine who I am.

If I want to change who I am, I change the accomplishments, either qualitatively or quantitatively. I try new things. I grow, I prosper and I may even thrive. But in the end I am still me, standing on the outside, looking at me from an external point of view.

To change this, I have to change my point of view. I need to adopt an internal viewpoint which describes me as I am, through characteristics such as being kind, gentle, caring, open-minded, big-hearted, alert, giving and so on. If these are my characteristics, then they define me more accurately than any external referents could. I can change externals; new house, office, car, job etc. But, can I really change the core of my being?

What I'm about to share with you something that some believe is a secret, but is, in fact, a universal truth. We are all Beings of Light. I am a Being of Light just as you are. We came to Earth for a purpose. We are to live that purpose on a day-to-day basis. Each of us struggles with who we are, what we have become and what we would like to become.

We want to change ourselves and this world for the better. To do so, we must refine our practices. These practices are accessible to Beings of Light whose earthly purpose is self-discovery through accomplishments and new beginnings. But here, we are again talking about external validation. You can see how we've come back around to this essential point.

As a Being of Light, I can change things that are mine to change, but can I change my state of being? Not surprisingly, the answer is No. That is a divinely bestowed state. I am a Being of Light. I am what I am.

So who am I then? Am I God incarnate? Or am I something else altogether? When we forget that we are Beings of Light, the question of "why am I here?" comes up again. Over and over, this question keeps repeating itself.

I believe that we are here for a purpose. Whose purpose is it? Is it God's purpose or is it mine alone? Do I define that purpose on my own, or do I reach to the Divine within for clarification and direction? We are here for a reason, and it is our responsibility to discover the unique purpose our life holds.

The Divine will direct us, but be assured the directives will be subtle. Each of us has a certain collection of possibilities before us that we can activate. Those that we choose to act upon will determine a specific direction which will help to define us within the context of our Divinity. It is our choice as to how we direct our lives.

We're here for a purpose. That purpose is flexible and dynamic. That purpose will unfold before each of us in a manner that is unique to our character and circumstances. We are directed to our Heart Center which contains all the information we need. Our purpose is revealed to us through our feelings which emanate from within the Heart Center This answer invites us to move to the next stage of our evolution which involves the expression of that inner you, the Being of Light that you are, the God Force within.

Discovering who you are, essentially, is that purpose. We are here for a purpose. We are alive with such purpose and that purpose expresses itself through our Being. This is a frustrating yet humbling realization.

The process of self-discovery requires that we pay attention to our feelings when we express characteristics such as kindness, caring, curiosity, open-mindedness and more. Otherwise, we miss uncovering who we are.

Let your purpose be that which you express, as yourself, your inner being, which is you as a Being of Light. Your God Self shapes you, guides you and prods you along. God, our Creator is also here to guide you in your quest to identify and actualize your purpose. This is God's purpose as well.

This is very important. This divine mentoring comes to us from within and guides us forward on our truest path. Each of us has the capacity to express this purpose in our communion with others, influencing their purpose as well as our own. This is our story, which includes helping others with their story as well.

16 – A Roadmap for Ascension

Before we can bring our full attention to Ascension, we must first elevate the Self within the human frame as the true center of the personality. No longer the ego, but the Self!

Why the Self?

As noted in our introduction, the Self is the human side of the Self-Soul equation that we are. We are representatives of the Divine (Souls) anchored in a human body that is directed by the Self as an extension of its divine purpose. Self and Soul inform each other so that the Self guides our human representation while being informed and nourished by the Soul, its divine counterpart.

The Soul ascends as the Self grows and expands on this plane. The Self is our grounding in the earth realm. The Soul is our link to the Divine. The Divine is All-That-Is and includes the Soul which is every individual Soul on this Earth.

To bring Self in line with Soul and the Divine we need a bridge. The Path of the Hero is the best representation of that bridge to the Divine. We use the Hero Path as a model for building our bridge and then crossing it. We call this our Bridge to Hope. Hope being the Divine and bridge being the link from Self to Soul. This bridge is an essential part of our path that we will construct.

What tools of bridge building do we require to help us connect Self to Soul? Inner communication, to be precise! Communicating with the Self—listening to Self via journaling—is one such bridge to Soul. There are others of course that come to us via the creative arts, such as music or painting. For our purposes, we will be focusing on journaling as the most widely accessible tool available to the majority.

Self always leads to Soul. Ego always leads away from Soul. Since you are reading this material, you are at a point in your development where you have to choose. Choose Self and you are on your way to Soul. Choose ego and you remain in 3rd dimensional consciousness which is separation from Source.

When we forego ego, we step onto the Self side of the bridge. The Bridge to Hope then becomes our bridge to Soul and Divinity.

You may have heard those claims that the Divine is right there where we left it. But just being told something like this does not necessarily translate into knowledge. However, firsthand experience can readily become knowledge, because knowing at a felt experiential level is the all-important key. What we acquire through our heart and feeling center transcends the ego and takes up residence within the totality of our being.

The Ego

The ego is a bump on the road that has to be negotiated. It must be seen for what it is—a frightened part of us that buys into separation and is hungry for power. The ego has become a distraction in our evolutionary process, a sticking point where many flounder. The ego represents the ultimate aspect of 3rd dimensional thinking. It repeatedly attempts to control fate, which is futile. Runaway egos lead to addiction and very often suicide, at the very least to grandiosity, authoritarianism and chaos.

The ego is the only part of us that truly dies when our physical body expires. At some level, the ego knows it is going to die. But it doesn't really believe it because it has no experience with dying. Remember, only experience is true knowledge. "Dying happens to others and not to me" says ego. So the ego directs you toward achieving greatness or accumulating money as a way of insulating itself against the truth of its finiteness. Some of us pursue greatness through education, as I did with my 3 degrees including a Doctorate in Psychology. Others pursue money as a way of personal validation and pushing off the inevitable finiteness of physical life.

Oftentimes these pursuits are about vindication rather than a true calling. They are usually propelled by feelings of inadequacy and negative self-worth which are covered over with strategies involving achievement, accumulation or power.

In my case I astonished everyone with my education, especially my parents, who I thought believed me to be inadequate. That was my self-judgment at work and not necessarily their perception. As mentioned above, many individuals seek grandiosity through the accumulation of money, like Madoff and his Wall Street cronies. Some pursue scientific greatness. I pursued university degrees.

These are cases where wonderful talents are used in the service of the ego and its need for self-aggrandizement. That is the state of the ego. It wants to dominate. No matter what you achieve or accumulate, it is never enough. Like with any addiction, there's an unending craving and the ego always wants more.

The Self wants to comply with the grander purpose that life has to offer. Our Self wants the true glory of self-sufficiency and its divine inheritance from the larger matrix. Self, in the beginning, knows at an unconscious level that it belongs to God. Self becomes aware of its divinity through our efforts at self-development and personal growth. Self communicates with Soul. Soul helps elevate Self until Self can see its true nature as part of the Divine matrix.

This is when evolution becomes conscious. Conscious evolution is our purpose at this time and the road to Ascension. We must rise above the petty circumstances of glory seeking and other side trips perpetrated by ego. These are only distractions designed to keep the ego in power. What truly matters is our being and our connection to All-That-Is. We need Self and Soul working together to actualize the Divine on the earth plane which we are all seeking.

To come out from our morass of pettiness and simplicity, we need to engage psychology, spirituality and mythology. We need all of these influences working together to help us move past ego so we can begin the work of healing and releasing the early dysfunctional influences that propped ego up and gave it the illusion of power. Taking our personal healing seriously means taking our life seriously. Moving from ego domination to self-acceptance and self-affirmation is the revolution necessary to fully engage the process of Conscious Evolution.

This doesn't happen until we reach that point where we know enough about ourselves to take the proverbial bull by the horns, by consciously choosing our destiny as it is informed by Soul. This is the process I have been engaged in for the past 20 years, since I wrote the first draft of my novel, *The Voice*. I am completing a process of connection, which is the felt experience of the Divine in my life.

This has been difficult because my ego would not let go easily. On the other hand, I would not let go of my ego until it felt safe to do so. Letting go of ego by stepping on the bridge that leads from Self to Soul is the proverbial "Leap of Faith." It is frightening to let go, but it is necessary to begin the process of Ascension. The ego is an anchor that must be released. It goes when you let it go, and not before. You cannot wish it away, you must demote it, and you cannot do that until you own it. Yes, this sounds like a contradiction, but that's how self-acceptance works. You must own every part of you before you can release or alter what no longer works.

In the process of "receiving" over the years, I learned to release my ego's influence little by little. I was always scared to let go completely. This is the Hero's Journey par excellence. Each of us has to take that step with our heart in our throat. When you stay focused on your goal of connecting Self to Soul, you will arrive safely.

Your ego knows that and will throw every anxiety provoking situation it can at you to keep you reliant upon it. Only by remaining focused and persevering with your personal and spiritual growth efforts, will you conquer that attachment.

What You Need to Know

Your ego is simply the frightened child within you, the part that may have been abused or simply scared in early life. It then chose to stay partially hidden as a matter of survival. Your anger or rage is the protective part of the ego alliance, and is analogous to mythology's guard dog Cerberus. Once your ego finds itself at the mercy of your continuous efforts to grow, it begins to see its end on the horizon. Your ego will fight tooth and nail because it views its descent from power as a death. Once you understand these dynamics, you will find it easier to let it go.

Your ego may kick up a fuss now and then from its new position on the perimeter of your being, but it will reveal itself as the frightened child it has always been. Your Self, now properly placed at the center of your life, will let it speak, through your journal perhaps, but never let it dominate again. Once you have broken the spell of the ego, there is no going back. Conscious Evolution is fully engaged and you are ascending at an accelerated pace.

Your Self, directed by Soul, will be your guardian and director from this point forward. Your Self will become more consciously aware of its divine heritage. You will begin allowing your decisions to be informed by Source. You will consult with that part of you more often, and your life will move forward with grace from that point on.

You will know that God, your Higher Self, is with you at all times, and that it does not live out there as an external referent, but actually lives in your heart, your feeling center, as has always been the case. This feeling based connection is the knowledge that you seek. That felt embrace is the reality of who you are on this plane, at this very moment. There are no other explanations. You are God, and God is You.

Building Our Bridge

Can you see this pattern we are talking about? We build our Bridge to Hope by our conscious choice. We align ourselves with All-That-Is by making Source the main focus and influence in our lives. We get to this point by relinquishing ego as the center of our life. Ego is always frightened. Ego goes to war because it is frightened. Ego accumulates wealth because it is frightened. Ego is driven by fear. Self is motivated by love. Which of these paths do you want to affirm in your life right now? The ego's path of fear, or the Self's path of love? You must decide.

Ascension is about bringing the Divine into material form while moving into greater realms of consciousness to meet Source. We and Source are reaching for each other. As mentioned, ego dominates in 3rd dimensional consciousness. Self and Soul dominate in 5th dimensional consciousness. Ascension is the process of moving from the 3rd dimension to the 5th by entering and negotiating the transitional healing and clearing stage of the 4th dimension. This 4th dimension is our spiritual adolescence. The 5th dimension is adult spirituality.

I will be using myself as a reference point as we document this process to show you what to expect along the way. It won't make your journey any less painful, but it will give you the courage to stay on track. You have nothing to lose but the pettiness of your ego and everything to gain from the gifts and talents available through your Self. You will express all that you are because your Self, no longer repressed by ego, will be free to explore and create. You will want to create because the Divine is your co-pilot, and creating is what God does.

Foundation

Our foundation for this process is spiritual psychology, as described in the hero myth at the beginning of this book.

Method

We need a linking mechanism to pull all of this together. That mechanism is communication with Self and Soul via journaling. We will be consulting with Soul at every opportunity through conscious journaling.

To begin, write a brief summary of your life story, identifying key experiences along the way that shaped subsequent decisions. This will give you a view of your path through life to this point. Again, I will be illustrating with my own life path.

Asking the Tough Questions
- How did you come to this Earth?
- What have been your life lessons?
- Who are your parents and what was their influence?
- What was your church or childhood religion?
- What drove you to pursue of self-help and personal growth?
- How did you arrive here at the doorstep of Ascension?

My Story
In my case I will be dealing with working class parents who used physical discipline and sometimes violence to deal with their children.

I will address the Catholic Church, its influence on me and my parents, and my ultimate rejection of it as a crippling entity that actually denies access to the Divine.

My early pursuits included a commitment to self-help and the field of psychology as a way out of the pain of my youth, followed then by my years as a therapist.

My early beginnings connected me with Guidance, assisted in letting go of ego and fully embracing Self, Soul and Source.

I developed a personal understanding of why I came to be here on planet Earth, my chosen circumstances and my chosen parents.

A growing understanding of all these influences evolved into my life path and my undying commitment to Source throughout my journey.

With the help of my Guidance, I will breathe life into every facet of this process.

Now Is The Time!

Wanderings

What is it that makes us wander the world looking for what is so often right under our noses? Does our self-esteem require us to make grandiose gestures, superlative plans or a great show of ourselves in our efforts to contact the Divine?

The Divine doesn't care about any of this, and there is no reason for it. We are not guided by the Divine to exhibit grand gestures. We are guided to show our Heart, our Soul and our Selves in all that we do.

The Divine does not need you in Tibet or on top of Mount Everest. The Divine wants to see you revealed through you. What you say, feel, conceive or create is a more accurate and amazing reflection of who you are. As a creation of the Divine, you are imbued with the ability to create yourself anew and the world around you. This is your choice.

There is no need for lengthy pilgrimages when you can journey within to discover that you can already express the ideal that you are, where you are. Show your true Self. That is a worthy and impressive accomplishment.

17 - Journaling

Journaling is empowerment through self-awareness. It is a process by which you meet your needs for emotional and spiritual cleansing. You will record the ideas, thoughts and emotions that you currently find distracting. Journaling helps you remove the cobwebs from your thinking and analytical processes.

This process is about balance. Journaling gives you access to your inner thoughts and feelings, and helps you remove them from the cluttered storehouse of your unconscious. You will clearly see where you are going from day to day, what you are thinking and what you need to focus on as your growth unfolds.

The world opens up to you when you start journaling because your unconscious receives the message that you are ready to access information from your inner world. Self-empowerment, through self-knowledge, is about entering your world of unconscious activity where you have stored past traumas, hurt feelings and un-examined life events. When you're open to this process, you will uncover much about yourself that has heretofore remained hidden.

Journaling is not a shortcut to immortality or creative writing. It is simply an access point to your inner life where valuable information about who and what you are can be uncovered.

Disregard any other ideas you may have about journaling, especially those that suggest you have to write creatively on some specific subject. This is not the case. Journaling is about self-revelation. It is about bringing your unconscious Self to conscious awareness. Only by knowing what you believe in and acting on that information can you make choices for a better life.

The conditioning you received in your early years is still active within you, even if it no longer makes it to conscious awareness. That's what repeating patterns of behavior are about. We are being driven by a part of us that believes in unquestioned and outdated ideas. Once you see these patterns and the ideas that drive them, you can interrupt your automatic responses and make new choices.

Prepare yourself for a rough ride at times. The unconscious protector-controller aspect of your ego will try to steer you away from recognizing this inner activity. This part of you has a big investment in remaining hidden and will resist your pursuit of self-honesty and increased awareness.

In the end, you will acquire what you want because your submerged Self wants to surface. It wants the same level of freedom that you desire. You and your deeper Self will become collaborators on that front. The old guard, the protector-controller, will put up resistance because it is about to lose its job. Successful journaling requires you to listen to all the voices within, including the ones resisting the process. So when that resistant part is active, put it on the page.

Your resistance will hiss and snarl at times of change. Let it do so in your journal. You'll see this happen time and time again. It's a struggle for every part of you. When you choose to make a change, even when that change is for the better, that decision upsets the old balance. Let the resistance have its say in your journal. Only then can you set it aside and resume your forward motion.

Once you begin this process and engage in it regularly, your journaling will become self-activating. Whenever something inside you clamors for attention you'll find yourself reaching for the journal to let it out. Whatever needs your attention put it on the page--good, bad or indifferent. Do not edit or deny what's begging for attention. You'll learn that these negative parts of you are frightened. Once those feelings are out and acknowledged, you will immediately calm down.

Journaling is a powerful process of self-communication. It will activate itself time and again as you become accustomed to using it. Begin simply by recording your feelings. Let your inner Self tell you what is going on inside. Do not edit or distort. Just record! Ask yourself feeling questions. We are all quite capable of rationalizing our thoughts and feelings rather than experiencing them.

When you ask feeling questions, listen for feeling answers and write them down. Your protector-controller will try and dissuade you from going too deep. Feeling questions help you sidetrack that resistance.

"How do I feel about . . . .?" will help you reach the center of any difficulty while bypassing the guardian at the gate to your interior life. You will discover things about yourself that are truly amazing, secrets you've never revealed to anyone. You'll uncover regrets you have about past experiences, hopes you hold for your future and secret desires that you have never been willing to admit to. This is your chance to do all that adventurous excavating while clearing your emotion and feeling center of psychological debris. This will be a time of great learning accompanied by great frustration. It's all part of the package and that is to your benefit.

Do not give up on your recording practices once things start to calm down. Your journaling sessions will become smoother as time marches on, and you'll be better equipped, in terms of emotional and spiritual strength, to handle each and every crisis that comes your way.

Journaling takes you to the well of personal wisdom from where all answers emerge. Eventually, you will find yourself confronted with the deity that is you, your own Holy Soul. It will reveal much about who you are and help you secure the connection with the Divine.

In time, you will trust that connection so completely that you will begin to access it often, especially when big decisions are on the table. At this point, you will see yourself as co-creator with your God Source and happily utilize that guidance for every aspect of your life.

That is the power of journaling. It puts you in touch with your essential Self, which puts you in touch with Source, the Divine within. We are part of that Divine Matrix and we are all enriched by this connection.

Let journaling be your friend from this point forward.

Opposites

God says, "Let there be soil." God says, "Let there be rain." God says, "I know what I want. I want men and women to populate this Earth I've created out of soil and rain."

This is the Divine's way of defining opposites. Bringing two differing and opposing forces into an equation provides tension. That leads to a scenario of dominance and subjugation, when two forces come together as undercurrents to a new reality.

With tension, there is conflict. Conflict can be resolved and needs to be resolved. This fosters our growth and evolution to become all that we are meant to be. When you mix soil with water you have created the conditions for growth. Add the necessary seeds and the Earth reveals multiple avenues for growth, ours included, of course.

Are the men and women of Earth really opposites? Of course not! They are more alike than they are different. Each gender realizes this as they get to know their so-called opposite. That is why communication through interaction is so important.

Opportunities for sharing are defined as occasions where you hold exchanges with one another. Then you have something to discuss that is real, not some invention from your projected fantasy about who or what the other is. Real communication always reveals the truth about ourselves, first, and then about those we are eager to know and understand.

Men and women will mingle, get to know each other better and share that understanding within and among their own groups. Knowing women as they truly are is a good idea for men, as is the corollary for women. This is a challenge. It is an avenue to understanding our Selves as well.

18 – Childhood

We start this process of self-discovery with childhood. This is where most of our emotional baggage comes from. Many of us were damaged in childhood, some more intensely than others. Some of us were traumatized later in life such as adolescence or young adulthood. We typically have issues stemming from our early beginnings that lead us to therapy or the self-help section of the bookstore.

At the end of this chapter you will start journaling about your childhood; what you remember, what you felt, what you have held on to and have released, what you have yet to uncover, and what you still have to resolve.

Ascension is a spiraling process with evolutionary steps cycling over and around each other. It is a repetitive, cleansing process. We go over surfaces as many times as necessary to fully cleanse ourselves. So it is with our childhood issues, or any trauma we may have experienced throughout the course of our lives. We begin this process of journaling and repeat as often as necessary. As we progress through the various stages of our life, we will see childhood issues re-emerging for a second, third and perhaps even a fourth look. There is no wrong way to do this. We perform all of the steps we must and repeat as necessary until the job is done.

Freeing ourselves of childhood trauma is a must for Ascension to occur. This is where different aspects of the hero myth apply. We must look at ourselves in ways we have never done before. We have to peer into the dark corners at previously overlooked crevasses that have become home to disowned parts of us. We may move at a snail's pace sometimes, but we will get through this process faster than we can imagine, certainly faster than trying to ignore it.

Healing and growth begin with us. They also end with us. We are the alpha and omega of our individual lives. Uncovering our hidden realms and the damage therein is job one. Ascension cannot occur without this process having taken place first. We need to examine ourselves fully before we can move on to the higher dimensions of being.

Our work is sacred. It is undertaken with the full knowledge that we are the caretakers of our individual lives. We are the ones who signed on for certain childhood dramas so we could have the necessary lessons to prepare us for Ascension. Rather than seeing this as simply a process of cleansing to be rid of certain things, let's view it as a series of lessons we gave to ourselves prior to incarnating in preparation for the undertaking of our current task.

If our incarnation is no accident, then neither is the work we chose to encounter upon our arrival on the earth plane. Why we chose these lessons is a different matter than why we must view them at this time. They are, after all, surprises that we issued forth prior to taking up our position here on this earth. As it is now time to ascend, we must unwrap and bring forth all our gifts so we can see our true selves, our Higher Selves, and what we chose to learn. Pretend it is Christmas and you are unwrapping the gifts you placed under the tree, in preparation for this moment of uncovering.

This is where we begin to communicate with our Higher Self. This Self has dealt us a hand that we willingly accepted in view of the life circumstances we were to negotiate. We knew, at some level, what we each needed to actualize for our individual Ascension. We knew what psychological blocks would give us the most trouble, and we knew what strengths would be required to achieve our exalted state. We put this process into motion and now we are in the game uncovering the results as we need them.

Let us examine every dimension of our experience. Let us take pen in hand and begin dialoguing with our Higher Self in order to allow it to guide us forward.

This is why we must release our ego from its place of dominance in our lives. Our ego only knows 3rd dimensional reality. We are moving through the 4th dimension with our main destination being 5th dimensional consciousness. Now is the time to take this process in hand and proceed with our uncovering tasks.

The Process
Let us examine the circumstances of our birth:

Take pen in hand and begin writing about your perceptions of your parents: 1) who they are or were; 2) what they stood for; 3) what they did for a living; 4) what their values were; 5) whether they practiced a religion; 6) if so which one; 7) if not, then why not; 8) if they were attentive to you, or not; 9) if they were abusive to you and how. This is about your recollections and how you interpreted things. This is not a criminal investigation seeking absolute facts. You need to know how you reacted to your environment, how you felt about it and whether or not you felt safe, or insecure.

Write out everything you can recall about your parents during your childhood. How you saw them. What they meant to you. Were they accessible? Were they remote? Did they love you openly? Were they neglectful? Were they happy? Were they sad or angry? Did they separate or divorce? And how any or all of this affected you?

This is your homework for this first stage of inner exploration. You may notice themes as you write. You may begin seeing these themes again and again as you proceed through your childhood up to your early teen years. Stop there. Journaling to ages 12 to 13 will suffice for now. There will be more for you to do later.

Now, you are mapping your childhood, identifying key components of experience and demarcation points where life changed for the better or worse as you progressed along your path. You are not ready for more than that at this time. We recommend that you not read ahead until you feel satisfied you have completed this challenge.

Engaging in this process places you within the 4th dimensional stage of transition in this Ascension experience. This is part of your spiritual adolescence, replete with all the wanderings, misgivings and apprehensions that come with any transitional state. Things may be convulsive for a time, or they already are and you're finally starting to get some answers.

As you go through this period of transition, you will obtain a better understanding of who you are today. Soon, you will glimpse a view of who and what you are about to become, and that's where the fun begins.

There is no limit on how much you need to write. But these directions should prompt you to write for several days before you come back to the book for the next stage in this process.

Begin now and rejoin us here when you feel done with this part of your exploration. All heroic journeys begin at the same place. And that is exactly where you are at this moment.

My Childhood

I won't go on with lengthy descriptions of my youth because that's the personal part of the journaling process, the part you reserve for yourself. For the purposes of this book, the summaries I have offered will suffice to serve as examples to your own explorations. Offering myself as an example also lets you know that I have lived what I am describing and am still living it to this day. What I have presented here is an outline of my early influences to which I can make reference along our journey together. Since I have done these exercises on my path so many times now, I know this territory well.

As mentioned, use this as a template for your own self-explorations. But do go into great detail for every dimension you bring up. Remember, this is personal self-exploration work. Nobody needs to see what you are doing unless you choose to share those details. This is for your own enlightenment and personal understanding. You are doing this for your Self!

What did I conclude from my childhood?

Being at odds with your Self is an awful state to be in. You succeed at something and feel good for a while. You mess up in the tiniest way and you condemn yourself for days on end. You waver back and forth between accomplishment and condemnation. You are never good enough and that undercurrent has become your default standard of reference.

Sometimes you hate yourself overtly, but secretly believe you are special. At least you hope you are, because that gives you something to hold on to. You have fantasies about your importance.

The hurt and pain of childhood can last a lifetime if we don't make the effort to uncover the damage, heal ourselves and then let go. We cannot let go of what has not been owned. And owning it means feeling it. That's what this process is all about. We are feeling our losses so we can let them go. But we have to get acquainted with our defenses before that can happen and that is a challenge in itself.

Defenses are what we erect to protect ourselves from the slings and arrows of early childhood abuses, on up to adolescence. At that point we tend to ingrain them more deeply because of the onslaught of put downs coming from our peers. We are emotionally sensitive at this time and we try hard to employ our defenses to mitigate the pain coming at us from so many directions. There are times when we thought we failed and went home in tears; at other times when we felt hurt we simply lashed out at others.

We bring the results of our childhood experiences into our adolescent relationships and trade hurtful barbs with each other. No wonder there are so many suicides at this age. As already pointed out, this level of hurt can be downright fatal for some, with so many stories of adolescent suicide coming out in news reports these days. Most of us do make it through this period, but more often than not, we do so with a collection of neurotic tendencies we can now write volumes about as we look back through a purging process such as this.

And that again is part of your homework. Use this template as a model for erecting the framework of your childhood experiences. Fill in the blanks as new memories surface. Don't rush this process; it is crucial to your success at Ascension. I have been doing this for over 30 years and written thousands of pages about my childhood and how it affected me. Don't be surprised if you lay out a few hundred.

For those of you well acquainted with this process, get down the broad strokes with enough detail to be able to reference those key points in your life. For those of you just beginning I encourage you to take all the time necessary to delve into every nook and cranny of your early years and record everything you can remember and felt at the time.

Remembering and recording events and feelings from childhood is our foundation. Because this is where the stage was set for the lessons we came to learn. And those lessons must be completed before Ascension can ever happen. We cannot move into the 5th dimension of consciousness while still dragging unresolved 3rd dimensional issues. It is simply that important that we get this part right from the very beginning.

19 - Our Feeling State

Do you ever wonder what it would be like to have a life without feeling? Would it be possible to enjoy anything at all? Could one be happy or sad without being in touch with their feelings? I would have to say that's an impossible paradox.

Our feelings are our life blood. They fuel the energy with which we create. They tell us about our state of being, be that happiness or sadness, and everything in between. Our feelings are a large part of our life. They drive us, enliven us and jostle us into action.

We are our feelings at every stage of our life. We are sadness when we feel discouraged, hope when we see reasons to be optimistic, and all those emotions that fall in between. Our feelings tell us who we are. They give meaning and value to our existence, our relationships, our dreams and aspirations. They tell us where we are, moment to moment, in our ongoing cycle of being.

However, we are not only our feelings as we experience them, but our understanding of our feelings. We know, for example, that to lie will result in feeling guilty. We have a choice, to lie or not to lie, and then experience the consequences as a result. Sometimes the truth brings its own pain. Is that a reason to lie? Of course not! No matter what the cost, being truthful is ultimately our best choice.

That's the way it is with feelings. They come and they go. They can be fleeting or intense. Feelings are always telling us what's in our hearts and invite us to pay attention. We can deny or attempt to block our feelings as many individuals do. But then you miss out on a lot of important information, about yourself and what currently requires your attention.

Feelings can take us up or down. They can move us into places we've never been by their simple invitation and our natural curiosity. Curiosity coupled with feelings adds drama to our explorations. Feelings enhance memory, and vice versa; they make some events and interactions stand out because of the quality they add to those experiences.

We have feeling adjectives such as happy, sad, angry, hurt, elated, depressed, grumpy, excitable and more. We have descriptive language for our feelings which can be associated with physical displays. "You look tired" or "you are glowing today." Our face reveals feelings as does our body language. Poets use language to describe different states of feeling, creating pictures for our imaginations. Our body, vocal tone and other signs reveal even more about how we are feeling. Happiness can display itself as an open and animated physical state with words to match. Denial is equally visible as a stiff posture, arms crossed and glazed look, despite language that belies it. Our body will tell the truth, even when our words do not.

Can we run away from our feelings? We can, to a certain extent. This happens all the time. People grieving losses, remembering a bad time in their lives or denying their inner reactions to a traumatic event; these are all examples of hiding from one's inner experience. Many individuals have learned to block the flow of feeling energy from coming into awareness by blocking their inner core. Such forms of repression can be quite crippling. This happens when intense emotional reactions push us to the edge of our capacity to accept such pain.

Our Self, which experiences all of this, is the center of our feeling nature. Feelings must be accepted and felt before we can deal with them. In fact, identifying their nature and what they are trying to tell us is essential to understanding our current state of being. Without that connection and flow of emotional energy, our simple defenses can easily be overwhelmed. We then find ourselves lashing out at people who have nothing to do with that feeling state. Awareness, acceptance and processing of our feelings are essential to maintaining personal wellbeing and good relationships.

Feelings provide information about who and what we are, where we stand in our personal evolution, and where we are going from this point forward. Rehashing unhealed feelings is a way of staying in the familiar and limiting ourselves. Moving through our feelings supports our growth. Accepting and working through our feelings and experiencing them allows us to release their hold on our psyche. When meeting their need to be identified and expressed we become free of their negative influences in our life.

A few lines on a journal page may be all that is required to release an emotional blockage. It can be a valuable starting point which will begin to indicate to us what additional actions may be required for their release. Like children, feelings can cling to us until acknowledged and allowed to tell their story. We can release feelings only after we've accepted them, at which point they can be safely expressed and released. We continue to experience and process additional feelings in the same manner.

Feelings are our allies. They tell us who we are by their energy and flow, and by their relationship to our current state of being. We are relieved of tension when feelings are accepted and allowed to flow through us. Some feelings will propel us toward adventures we may not have thought of before. They help us grow, and expand our vision of the world and our place in it. When understood, feelings and emotions provide us with a map of our interior life.

The feeling part of us holds us dear. It reminds us we are loved and informs us when we are wounded and need care. At every juncture of life experience, a feeling can inform us of our importance and value. We help children grow by validating their feelings. We can help ourselves flourish in the same manner.

Celebrate what you feel, even the pain, because all feelings will move through you. Once a difficult feeling is acknowledged, you will know you have survived a challenging experience. When joy presents itself, you will be able to soar with that as well. Like all things in life, feelings are transient. They tell us a story about ourselves and invite us to grow. To our feelings we must go and without reservation. They imbue our lives with meaning and that enriches us all.

20 – Adolescence

Adolescence is one of the most tumultuous experiences in an individual's life and is particularly well noted in western culture. It represents one of the strongest demarcation points in an individual's personal evolution. Moving from childhood to adulthood is no easy task. Adolescence is a road of trials.

There is enormous confusion at this time. The need to focus on one's growth clashes with the desire to hold onto childhood. A young person is compelled to move forward, not by conscious methods, but by the sheer pull of physical maturation.

The young person's body is preparing itself for sexual activation. Their mind is far behind in what that means. Moving from crawling on the floor to standing erect and walking is nothing compared to this crucial step.

We are required to abandon our childhood and leave the innocence that came with it. Our bodies are signaling that something magical is happening. We are changing at an alarming rate. We are like young birds shedding their childhood feathers and developing the new feathers that permit flight. This is a leap of monumental proportions.

There are casualties along the way. Some individuals simply refuse to grow and hang on to childish dreams. Others navigate the transition from childhood to adolescence to adulthood rather willingly and do so with grace and aplomb.

Many of us get caught during some of these transitions, stuck in some dilemma having to do with earlier experiences. If you've been molested or physically abused, you will have greater difficulty. The traumas and abuse experiences that were driven underground in childhood now clash with the issues and demands of adolescence. Such early ruptures, having been unattended, will make the transition into adolescence and young adulthood more difficult for many.

Many of us don't make it through unscathed. Adolescence is that period when neurotic strategies, including defenses, are adopted in a vain attempt to secure some measure of control over what is happening within and without. Adaptations are based on the lingering effects of certain childhood traumas and the emerging demands of adolescent maturation.

We refer to this as baggage in psychotherapy, the baggage of unresolved issues that have been piling up. Childhood issues continue to press for attention. Adolescence steps up and attempts to overrule those so called childish demands. This is often seen in the conflict of adolescence.

Adolescent demands are primary as young people push and prod each other into action. They call each other names and deliver shaming and hurtful judgments to each other. On a more positive note, young people do challenge each other to grow despite the gauntlet of teasing and putdowns. They also strive to distance themselves and individuate themselves from the adult population. This is another part of the story that makes this transition so difficult and volatile.

A number of things begin to happen at this stage. Psychological defense mechanisms evolve and take a foothold. If we are uncomfortable with what we are learning or have learned about our Self, we block it out. On other occasions we simply deny it or project it onto others. This is the beginning of avoiding self-responsibility.

In adolescence, we don't have a clear picture of who we are, so we take whatever steps necessary to protect the vulnerability of a fragile ego. We cannot fully grasp the essence of who we are just yet, so we project an ideal of who we would like to be. A young person's feelings are easily hurt. Friendships can be broken in an instant. And, the pressure for sexual activity is upon us.

Adolescence often involves a mix of glory seeking and self-protection for both boys and girls, with each gender manifesting those ends in a unique fashion. This mish mash of conflicting agendas feels like you are walking through a gauntlet every day of your young life. Eventually there will be peace. But long before that arrives, there is the pain of growing up and facing all the demands this transitional stage serves up.

Some of us become alienated from our parents at this time. They have adult privileges that we would like to access, but we are not permitted to execute just yet. We are impatient to get there, yet we are ill prepared for the accompanying responsibilities. We want more freedom, yet we are afraid of it. We want access to alcohol, yet we are unprepared for its effects on our underdeveloped bodies, minds and emotions. We may want to consummate a relationship, yet we have no idea what that involves, or what are the inherent dangers. We want what we are not yet ready for simply because it is there.

Our parents guide us as best they can, yet they remain bewildered all the same. Our conflicting demands and runaway emotions are a challenge for them as it is for us. Neither our parents nor we know which way to turn.

There is drama in adolescence, which few of us are prepared to navigate. We tend to stumble along and react to our circumstances rather than preview and consider what might happen with various choices. Try as we might, we often succumb to the temptations of others who have already been experimenting. Many of us leap into situations that can have catastrophic consequences.

We are wary and bold, often at the same time. We try new experiments because we feel pressured by our peers to take the chance. Oftentimes these experiments are replete with sorrow and shame. We regret our actions after the fact. Hopefully, the circumstances we were engaged in were not fatal.

We try hard to grow out from this storm of conflicting demands. Yet, we are subject to forces beyond our conscious control. Aside from our changing bodies, our expanding and developing thought processes and our growing interests begin to reveal that life can be lived in many different ways. We see what other cultures do for their children and start questioning the authority figures in our own lives. Our churches and other institutions often instruct us to resist certain behaviors as taboos without defining what that means, and our parents often nod in agreement.

All around us is a whirlwind of psychological and emotional activity. Defenses are being developed and installed. Lies are rehearsed so we can look good in another's eyes. Having the right gadgets, the right food, the right clothes and the right friends are the keys to success at this stage. Acquiring a driver's license is a major coup for many. These are not particularly great successes in the larger scheme, but they are significant markers toward adulthood.

Parents are delighted when we make it through and start talking about realistic hopes and aspirations, career choices, colleges to attend and matters they consider important. Our affairs of the heart tend to settle down into some routine as we gain confidence and experience with dating. For some, the idea of relationships won't be explored until later. Talk of sexual activity is kept private, whether one is involved or not, and usually only shared with a few close friends.

Parents are relieved to see their teens settling into new roles as young adults. But, the miscarriages of childhood are still with us and these will need to be resolved. Added to these are the bumps and bruises of navigating the adolescent gauntlet, often resulting in another host of issues that will require our attention.

We remain adolescents for some time to come, well into our 20s these days. But, the signs of emerging adulthood are showing, at least on the surface. We have jobs. We have cars. We have many friends. We have goals. We have arrived at a place where our parents feel they can recognize and trust us again.

In adolescence, there are many secrets. These are now ours to carry. Some will be shared. Many will not and become the undercurrent of irrational conclusions about what life is and who we are. If these beliefs are pliable, they will shift with new information. But some of these ideas and beliefs are already set in stone, and won't easily budge until an active therapy process is engaged. Until then, we turn to our friends for information and guidance because they are going through the same sorts of challenges and have some understanding of what we're going through.

The Fly in the Ointment

What happened to those childhood traumas and hurts? Were they buried along with so many other issues from that early part of our lives? What happened to all those hurts and abuses suffered during adolescence, at the hands of our peers, and yes, friends? What happened to all those hurts and traumas we've been gathering since we arrived on the planet? Where are they now? They are still with us, buried deep in those psychological closets we were so careful to build to keep us from harm.

Yes, we navigated adolescence relatively unscathed. At least we'd like to think so. But, we picked up a few kinks along the way. These lie in our psychological closets that are filled with unresolved issues. Some of these may have been taken care of by appropriate interventions from parents, authority figures and friends. A good number of them, however, still sit there seething and seeking to be released. We come to a point where we cannot keep stuffing them into that unkempt closet.

Some of us seek help in the form of life skills training and counseling which may alleviate and resolve the pressures coming from old issues pressing to be noticed. There are numerous programs for teens and young adults these days, and they do help. We understand, more than ever, the need to share and unburden ourselves from the traumas of youth.

Not everyone is reached in time. Some of our generation escaped into suicide, more common than we'd like to believe. Many have engaged in the use of drugs and alcohol to escape from the realities they find overwhelming. Self-loathing and self-abuse are common for young people who then turn to various addictions in order to cope. Addictive behavior patterns, such as drug and alcohol abuse, serve to arrest emotional development. You cannot grow when you are stoned, drunk or obsessed with other behavior that numbs the senses and the mind. These individuals will remain adolescent in their reactions to life's demands no matter what their chronological age.

Those who take up the challenge of personal growth and seek the necessary help will eventually become masters of their own destiny. Those who made that choice are here today, reading this or some similar book, and are preparing for the next thrust in human consciousness development, which is the 5th dimension of enhanced conscious awareness.

Where We Are Now

We are now facing another type of transition to be negotiated, a spiritual renaissance, where our central Self takes over the helm to guide us through this next evolutionary step. We chose to be here at this time. We chose this very moment for our awakening. We chose to serve our divine nature in this particular fashion. We are preparing ourselves for ascension into the 5th dimension of consciousness. However, we can expect a backlash of negativity coming to us from those who are committed to remaining in 3rd dimensional density consciousness.

We now have the strength and the foresight to negotiate these challenges. Without those years of necessary self-examination and personal development, we simply would not be ready. Some of us will still choose to stay on the sidelines. Many of us, having come this far and having paid the price, will happily move forward, driven by that Divine Presence felt as urgings within our heart. It is time to actualize that connection and anchor those expansive energies into this earthly realm.

We feel the Divine within us and around us. This is our awakening as we are fully present in this new dimension of consciousness. We are now in a position of being able to receive all that the Universe can deliver. We feel a creative energy in our hearts and have recognized the internal beacon burning brightly within, lighting the way for future endeavors and adventures.

Self-Responsibility

Self-responsibility is now at the door. Cleansing angels are here to help. You chose this path, and today is cleanup day. At this point, we are all moving forward. We must say goodbye to the trappings of past traumas and hurts. In preparation for Ascension, we must be as fully honest with ourselves as we can be.

The **intent** to be honest will suffice for now. What needs to be addressed will come up as surely as the sun will rise tomorrow. We will acquire more of the essential tools that will help us delve into our early history and permanently say goodbye to our collection of unique kinks and psychological knots. Remember, we signed up for this. We are at the stage of cleansing prior to negotiating the new path ahead. This can be exciting.

We are, at this time, boldly stepping into the unknown. Our physical adolescence swept us along its thorny path. Now we are aware that we have chosen to be here and are fully committed to our personal growth, no matter where it takes us. On our heroic journey into this New Age, we are going where only scouts went before to discover the unknown land and chart the new path. We choose to travel this path, for our own benefit and so we can bring back the news of what lies ahead to those wanting to hear about our adventures.

We are the explorers and teachers of this new movement toward wholeness. We choose full conscious awareness, which includes our personal and direct connection to the Divine.

We can no longer carry our sorrows. They must be left behind. There may still be tears and challenges to negotiate, but we will be fully aware of the process. We will work our way through the pain and leave it behind as we progress. We have come to the end of being a victim of our past. That door will now be closed once and for all.

We are all on this voyage together. We are all reaching for the stars. Our happenstance experiences through childhood and adolescence served as foundation for the lessons we needed to learn. Now we know we are of the Light and members of the Army of Light. We are leaving our egos behind at this juncture. You will see how as we meet "The Players" in our inner world of psychodynamics. Those defenses and coping strategies that got us by earlier have to be relinquished so that the truth of whom and what we are can emerge once and for all.

We are Divinely created. We are cut from the whole cloth of the Divine and of humanity. We are One with All.

Exercise

Write about your adolescence in detail, as you did with your childhood. Write about everything you can remember, identifying themes and key turning points throughout this stage of your life.

If you can identify defense strategies or psychological blocks, then do so. Do not worry if you can't. Our next set of exercises will address this more directly.

Be as honest as you can. Remember, this is for you. Leave no stone unturned. This is key to what comes next for your personal unfoldment.

Passion & Purpose

Who are we, standing on this planet, looking for a place to be? Are we "forgotten ones" from a time gone by, a piece of human pre-history perhaps, that allows itself to unfold through the pages of time?

Are we here alone, or are we part of something bigger, larger than we could ever imagine? We are like children, looking out into the Universe, wondering about our purpose and why we are here now.

As children we had dozens of questions about who we were, our purpose and our origins. We often wondered why we were here while we marveled about this place called Earth. There were grasshoppers, butterflies, leaping frogs, crawling snakes, ponies, dogs and cats, all sorts of strange and wondrous things that we discovered each and every day. That was the period of investigating this amazing world in which we had landed. We wondered often, then, looking up at the clouds, with a blade of grass stuck in our mouths, or a flower tucked behind our ear, "who are we?" and "why are we here?"

We must have access to and gain an understanding of these fundamentals to feel truly alive and valuable. Looking back at our respective childhoods, we can see the passion in every day of our life, manifesting itself here, there and everywhere as we set about on our path of discovery. Somewhere along the line that flame of passion was diminished, not going out, but reduced to a small ember. We need to fan this ember to return it to that bright blue flame. Fires may come and go but our passion is forever.

Passion without purpose is like a car spinning its wheels with nowhere to go. Passion needs to be attached to purpose, to be drawn by it, so we can be enlivened and motivated to move forward. If we have no purpose, then how can we have passion? Even if it's as simple as collecting stamps, we still need passion to be motivated.

In the morning, when we rise, what gets us going? Some will say "fear of getting fired" or "not making that next mortgage payment," but passion is ever-present, getting us excited about the day ahead, the challenges we face, and the successes to which we aspire.

Perhaps you remember John Lennon and Yoko Ono in the early 70s, staying in bed in a Montreal hotel for several days to bring attention to an issue that concerned them . They were promoting peace, urging an end to all wars and used their notoriety to make their point. Their "lay-in" received worldwide news coverage. Our world is full of examples of people's passion motivating them to positive action for themselves and for others. How can we know what anyone is about without knowing their passion or purpose?

The passionate life is a worthy life. It's exciting, even breathtaking at times. We are so captivated by the things we love that we can sometimes run into walls while thinking about them. Just like mythology's siren call, we are drawn toward this signal that beckons and invites us. However, these promptings intend no harm and come to us from the inside as intuition and messages from our inner Self. These terms all refer to the same living entity, that pulse that lies within and throbs for only us to hear and feel.

It's an exciting time when we do finally hear The Voice. It announces the birth of a new era when we are less motivated by what goes on outside of us and more concerned with our inner life. This is where we know the gold is. This is our best possibility for future success. This inner guidance gives us direction. With direction we have purpose. This is where our passion is to be found.

Wisdom seekers and prophets throughout history have told us repeatedly that purpose lies within. There, inside our hearts, a blue ember of passion smolders for each of us. It holds our purpose and our future. Your passion and purpose are waiting for you.

21 – Meet the Players

Our psychological dramas come with a cast of players who have taken up residence in our inner world. Some of them are like devils and others like angels, both of whom portray our respective challenges. They are metaphors, like characters from mythology, which all seekers must confront as they undertake their journey to wholeness.

We are all exposed to similar forces at this level. Good and evil play their roles on our psychic landscape. They inform us about who we are and what we are about to become. We have arrived at a cleansing stage that requires a strong acquaintanceship with these players. Knowing them at a core level provides understanding of the roles they've been playing in our lives.

We did meet them, or more accurately, created them along life's way, through our childhood, adolescence and into adulthood. They've been with us from the very beginning. Now, finally, they are subject to our scrutiny and identification.

The Ego
The ego is that part of us that addresses life on the material plane. Encased in our body, it dies with the body. The ego's job is to supply information about our place in the world and our state of being. The ego is our data processing component which examines all the facts, both visible and tangible. It reacts to this information in what it considers the most appropriate fashion. The ego is capable of splitting off parts from itself as a result of trauma. It will engage in self-deception to protect a pseudo and false self-image. The ego does not rely on input from the Higher Self. In fact, the ego reacts negatively to input from the Higher Self and deems it false.

Protector-Controller

The protector-controller is part of the ego. It is designed to protect us from the "slings and arrows of outrageous fortune." It governs our daily duties as we consider who we are supposed to be. It is made up largely of parental and authority figure influences. Our ego and its protector-controller component exhibit the various defensive strategies we employ when being buffeted by a reality that we do not like, such as criticism and judgment. Religion is one of those authority voices. Any authority plays a significant role in our upbringing as they are a core part our childhood experiences. Authority voices, both good and bad, are designed to keep us on the straight and narrow.

A constellation of authoritarian forces impresses upon us a series of injunctions such as "do as I say." We learn to comply with these conditioning forces. Included here are parental influences, religious doctrines, social pressures and educational authorities.

We are conditioned to a series of measures designed to keep us compliant. Most of these involve not challenging existing authority. Non-compliance is often linked to such consequences as harsh judgment, criticism or outright abandonment. Sometimes our resistance, if engaged at all, is delivered in a passive-aggressive manner so we can appear compliant without actually acquiescing.

The protector-controller portion of our ego believes it is our guide and director. Only our ego accepts this as true. For example, when we get married the ego says "This is a good partner for me because of this or that reason," usually supported by parental and social authority influences. What neither they, nor we realize is that a whole host of forces, many of them unconscious, have been at play bringing these two people together.

These forces include our past in this life, past lives, lessons to be learned and agreements made prior to incarnating. These form the undercurrent of our various life dramas which are replete with unconscious actions. Therefore, the ego and its protector-controller component are merely bit players in most of our actions.

Observer Self

What we term as the observer Self is that part of us that stands outside the picture, like watching a movie, and observes the action around us and our participation in it. This part makes interpretations about what is going on, but it always runs the risk of colliding with the ego when it does. Staying objective is its best option. It functions best by being neither right nor wrong, but simply observing our psychodynamics, feeling states, erupting emotions and inner conflicts.

The observer Self acts as mediator between the different parts that you will want to engage in dialogue. When we dialogue with some part of us that wants attention, we can refer to the observer as "me" or "I." Again, this is the part of you that listens, makes interpretations and provides feedback to the sub-personality that is speaking. For example, if you want to dialogue with your hurt Self, your observer Self will be identified as "me" and the sub-personality in this case will be identified as "hurt Self."

In your journaling the observer Self is always "me", and the parts you are dialoguing with are given names, such as "hurt Self," "angry Self" or "scared Self"; whatever describes the dominant emotion or feeling. This is a matter of convenience so that these different parts of you are identified before you let them unload on paper in the presence of your observer Self. This is how you learn about your inner dynamics and identify your major players with their differing agendas.

The Self

The Self appears first as our inner child. It is our feeling nature which can be easily compromised in childhood. The Self is often driven underground by the strong protective tendencies of the ego. "If people are out to hurt me, then I shall hide" is a familiar mantra, and the protector-controller steps in to do the job.

Much attention was paid to this part of our inner dynamics in the 1980s. This period signaled the beginning of a large scale rescue effort to liberate the Self from its ego constructed prison. Books on co-dependence, the inner child, addictions recovery, sexual abuse healing, dysfunctional family life and overcoming shame and guilt hit the self-help book shelves. Authors like John Bradshaw, Melodie Beattie and Marianne Williamson sat down with Oprah to talk about their work on how to deal with the above noted issues.

Many of us were at war with our selves, trying to heal the ruptures in our psyche that had been identified in the 60s and 70s by writers such as Thomas Harris' *I'm OK, You're OK*, Eric Berne's *The Games People Play* and Fritz Perls' *Gestalt Therapy*. They and other notable practitioners introduced us to Transactional Analysis, Primal Therapy, Bioenergetics, Psychodrama and the Alexander Technique to name but a few. During this time we were told that feelings were less important than logic as the latter held all the answers to our various dilemmas as long as we remained rational. But before long practitioners realized that understanding feelings was crucial to healing old wounds and individuals were encouraged to stand up to their childhood abusers, be they parents, extended family, educators or clergy. This attention to feelings and family dynamics was where the recovery movement came to the fore. These practitioners, mentioned above in the first group, were the ones who exposed the dynamics of addiction and, subsequently, the very need to rescue and heal the feeling component within a suffering individual.

As a result, we have given our inner child its just due. We demonstrated to that part of us that we care and we value its input in our lives. We have said "no" to the deniers of feelings and "yes" to a very important dimension of our inner world. Self and inner child, we now know, are one and the same. They are the true center of the personality and our link to the

Divine. This is the link that had been broken during humanity's long journey through denial, the very rupture that occurred when rational thought was elevated over feeling. The disconnect from "feeling" was where we broke off contact with the Divine within, our Higher Self.

Misappropriated and jargonized religion, among other destructive forces, literally and figuratively beat that awareness out of us. As a result, we gave more power to Freud's "superego" persona, the inner representative of external authority. It became the authority within our individual personalities. Religion is ego masking itself as the caring link to our respective Gods. Religion is a business, often selling the false hope of redemption through specialized methods such as regular church attendance, confession and rote memorization of certain scriptures. The Catholic Church, for example, teaches you not to trust yourself because you are prone to sin. Trust them, the church authorities, instead, and they will show you the way back to the Divine. None of these strategies have sound psychological values and all of them lead to crippling neuroses, which exhibit as major conflicts with Self.

Contrary to its claimed mandate, most religion steers us away from our true center, the Self, and installs itself as the main connection to the Divine. As a business model, this has worked extremely well. In practice, religion divides us as a people and then pits us against each other under the guise that one religion is right and superior, and the others are wrong. How many wars are still raging today over this position? Individuals committed to their personal growth and spiritual awakening are saying goodbye to this form of tyranny and learning to reconnect with Source on the inside.

The true Self is far more flexible than religion would have us realize. While religion has cast many of us as sinners, the inner Self works quietly at maintaining and strengthening its connection with Source. The Self waits patiently as we work through the religious drama and subsequent obstacles we must overcome in order to retrieve and activate our central core. The world around us is mostly unaware of this action, especially the religious and educational authorities of our times. The Self rises once again, without fanfare and without notice, to become the central component of our lives as was always the intent. Our side trip into religion is coming to an end. We will soon be completely free to exercise our Divinity unencumbered by volumes of rules and regulations designed primarily to keep the masses in check and the controller authorities in power. Churches and religious institutions are simply an externalized version of our superego and protector-controller. Psychologically speaking, most religions are the dysfunctional authority systems of our times. They are responsible for mankind's cataclysmic separation from Self and God.

Defenses

The ego and its protector-controller dimension come with a plethora of defense mechanisms. Most of these are widely accepted as common for all human beings. Many are not inherently bad. Every culture has its associative ego defenses. We will summarize those that are most relevant to this discussion. Remember, since you are an active seeker and conscious chooser in your personal unfolding, your identification of ego defenses will help you release some of their grip. Individuals who are highly defensive simply would not be engaged in this type of self-awareness project.

There are many more defenses than those covered here. This brief list will suffice for our purposes. The fact that you are here reading this book means you have worked through a lot of your externally imposed limitations and you are eager to know the truth about yourself. You are at least ready for a major leap forward in self-knowledge and understanding. Most defense mechanisms derive their source energy from the protector-controller component of the ego. The ego always wants to maintain an idealized image of itself for the preservation of self-esteem - at least the illusion of self-esteem. Because when the trance is broken, when an individual is confronted with the nonsense of their presumed superior position, they default to a deeper belief which is typically a negative self-view marked by self-loathing.

We remain at the whim of our ego defenses until we choose to challenge our protector ego and unmask its hidden agenda. There is nothing inherently wrong with wanting to feel good about ourselves, but it serves us poorly to have an inflated view that is disproportionate to how we truly feel deep down. Any inflated ideal will leave us vulnerable to criticism and attack. The ego's hidden agenda is protecting the fragile Self within. While that Self is kept imprisoned by the ego's faulty logic, it cannot grow.

Projection and Blaming

This involves mentally pushing off onto others what is inherently our own perceived limitation and/or defect. It involves a one-sided ability to see in others what is dysfunctional and unhealthy in their behavior and attitudes, without noticing the very same thing at work in oneself. For example, an angry person may readily see anger and blaming strategies in others, but not in him or herself; this is projection. Having been victimized in childhood, one may engage in projection to disassociate from the negative defensive habits one adopted to survive. Blaming others for these negative characteristics is simply one way to avoid looking at ourselves.

Dissociation

Dissociation is a negative reaction of the ego and its protector-controller component. Our ego splits off a part of us—our feelings usually, and oftentimes, our memories as well—especially when one has been violated by a traumatic experience of abuse. It then sends this part of us underground (into the unconscious), away from conscious awareness. This is common for abused children, war veterans and victims of battery. Dissociation tends to occur with any event or component of experience that the ego deems too painful to handle. All ego defenses are about protecting the fragile Self within, the inner child, which, you may now understand, will be rescued and reclaimed through the heroic journey.

This splitting off occurs unconsciously and as a reaction to threat. It is a protective reaction that has long-range negative consequences in that we lose a key dimension of our being. Our recovery becomes one of reclaiming and reintegrating these lost parts of ourselves so we can return to wholeness.

Growing awareness of your inner dynamics sets the stage for your recovery. You make this happen by engaging in personal growth practices, by investigating past traumas, by finding the right Self-help book or by going into therapy, if necessary, in order to heal all wounds associated with early psychological trauma. Observer Self, which is you, assesses and analyzes the dysfunction, then sets out to identify and secure a remedy. There may be strong denial before this step is taken. But when you do engage in self-discovery and self-healing, the ego suspects it is on its way out and will likely deliver a backlash. Although you are not entirely aware of it yet, your Higher Self is beginning to lead you along and help you see what needs to be done, including how to deal with an acting-out ego.

All dissociations must be identified and corrected. Some schools of thought call this unconscious material our shadow side, which means unseen. The point of the recommended journaling dialogues is that any part of us can be made conscious. Only in so doing can we correct what was previously unseen. No part of us remains out of reach when we commit to our healing.

Numbing Out

Numbing out, a form of avoidance, is usually associated with drugs or alcohol, both of which clearly deliver this effect to the body and mind. Numbing out also occurs with overwork, compulsive involvement in some activity such as gambling or in situations where an individual simply tunes out not to hear criticism or challenges to their world view. People numbing out look like they are in a trance where they can't hear or feel what is being addressed. It's a form of denial through the withdrawal of awareness from one's physiology, one's mental acuity and one's feeling state. It is avoidance of an unpleasant reality that one does not want to confront, feel and deal with. There are many cases where this is done consciously; there are many more where this has developed into an unconscious conditioned reaction.

Denial

Denial and numbing out are closely related. The strategy of denial is in evidence when a person automatically rejects thoughts, feelings, needs, wishes, or criticisms that they don't feel capable of dealing with consciously. This defense strategy is often linked to the idealized self-image we discussed earlier. In some cases it is an outright rejection of widely accepted facts. For example, when smokers are told that smoking causes cancer and ultimately leads to death, they will cite studies that repudiate the claim, or suggest that it is an exaggeration and that many smokers die of old age.

Accepting the truth about smoking would mean losing their favored addiction, which they are not prepared to give up. This plays well with any activity or process that has verifiable objective consequences but which the denier has chosen to ignore. We've all seen examples of this with relationships and other forms of addiction. Denial is primitive and tends to dissipate as we continue our journey inward. Denial, as an impediment to self-discovery, is soon overrun by the truth we are seeking.

Rationalization

Rationalization is a favored activity of the ego while in protective mode. With our smoking example above, rationalization is the tool employed when clinging to the untenable evidence that the addiction is not dangerous. Rationalizations are often called upon to protect one against criticism or judgment. Rationalization is a process of making excuses with the end goal of not having to change one's behavior or attitude. Rationalizations are also used to minimize the value of goals we once deemed important, like passing a critical exam as an example. Rather than feel disappointed or upset with ourselves for not having made the appropriate effort, we deem the event as unimportant. At some level we know we are making excuses and rationalizing because deep inside we often remain unconvinced of our own argument.

Compensation:

When traumatized in childhood, we often compensate by erecting a false Self, an image of who we would like to be and how we want others to see us. This strategy is often 180 degrees away from what we've already concluded about ourselves at a deeper unconscious level. For example, being denigrated and made to feel irrelevant during childhood can manifest later in an attitude of superiority to compensate for the early conditioning of being told we are useless. Such negative judgments are always painful and unbearable for children who, either give up altogether, or try to prove the judgment wrong by overcompensating in everything they do. Racking up accomplishments is one way to support the superiority facade. What gets lost in this approach is the true value of those accomplishments that one does not pause to enjoy.

Self-Deception

At this point we can safely state that all defense strategies are a form of self-deception. Defense mechanisms are protective measures that seem to work in the short term but really leave you wanting and vulnerable. There's always a part of you that knows the truth or, more accurately, knows what your deep-rooted limiting beliefs are. This is why a commitment to self-examination and inner exploration is necessary to get to the truth of your own being. You cannot change a false belief, good or bad, until you bring it out into the light.

Full self-disclosure is the only way to wholeness and Ascension. The pain of low self-esteem and childhood trauma give way to the joy of authentic self-discovery. This approach will lead you to the gifts you've been missing while engaged in self-deception. Every part of your self-discovery process is a step closer to actualizing your true Self. You will lose the pain of undisclosed traumas, false conditioning and negative beliefs drilled into you before you could judge for yourself. By challenging old ideas about yourself, you are gaining a clear understanding of your authentic Self. Abundance, love and positive self-worth are the gifts of your Soul. Living falsely and feeling defective is what your ego protector hangs on to. Becoming aware of this brings you back to making a better choice. Now you are regaining personal power.

Additional Characters

Hurt Self

The hurt Self is an aspect of our inner child. This part of us contains all the psychological and emotional injuries we've suffered since childhood and never completely worked through. This part of us is easily hurt again and again, despite our use of defense strategies. It's only through liberating the wounded child within that we help it gain strength and grow to the point where incoming volleys of criticism can be seen for what they are, someone else's negative attributes being projected onto us. As we reclaim our childhood traumas and their consequences, we can grieve our wounds and gain real strength with every healing step we take.

Angry Self

Our angry Self is reminiscent of the ego's protector-controller but more related to our inner child while behaving like the guard dog, Cerberus, from mythology. In this typical hero myth, the hero or heroine, as an observer

Self, goes into the underworld to rescue the inner child who is chained to a wall and protected by a vicious guard dog (our anger or rage). Immediately feeling the threat, the guard dog begins snarling and lunging at the intruder who wants to rescue the trapped child.

The hero assesses what has to be done to make rescue a success. Upon arrival in the underworld, the hero surveys the scene and calls for help which arrives in the form of a representative of the Divine, such as a Goddess, who then acts as a spiritual coach while bringing a sense of grace and calm to the situation at hand.

The hero is shown that attacking the dog will increase the threat to the imprisoned child. Only by calming the guard dog and allowing it to trust the hero can the latter proceed to rescue the child without risk of injury. The fact is that the child and the guard dog are one. And the angry part must be appeased before the frightened child can be saved. The hero learns that the chained child actually controls the dog. It's that part of the angry inner child that needs to gain trust in our intentions before it can allow the dog to surrender. Remember, we abandoned our inner child early in life when we were traumatized and abused by our caretakers. This part of us has very little trust when we first come back to retrieve it. But they do want to be rescued, and that makes our attempt viable.

This example illustrates an important function of our psychodynamics. All parts of us, even those we consider ugly or frightening, must be heard and accepted before we can move to our next level of being. Slaying the dog, or dragon if you prefer, increases the likelihood of more terror and angst, and leaves a critical situation unresolved. This is why wars breed more wars. When an individual or group is physically attacked, they will want to retaliate. At the level of ego, this appears to be the only course of action.

Transcending this ego-dominated scenario becomes necessary for the vicious cycle to end and healing to occur. We must make peace with all the players within our psychodynamics and bring them together to work for our common good. Then we can graduate to the level of multi-dimensional consciousness. And that's why we're here, to take the next step in our human evolution, by a process we call Conscious Evolution.

There may be other players inside your defensive structures. Having come this far, you will be able to name them yourself. What is important is that the different dimensions they represent are brought together and they are all nourished with affection rather than attacked and continuously rejected. Remember, our defenses are simply acts of disowning parts of ourselves by externalizing them, blaming others or engaging in denial. This is at the heart of victim thinking. The ego always wants to defend itself against "them" so it can remain in power and keep us busy with fruitless distractions. Remember, if all these forces are yours to begin with then you have choices to make. Do not continue rejecting aspects of yourself. Take ownership of all of whom and what you are.

These self-created defenses, for protection and safety, came about as a reaction to real stressors in our lives. You never made a conscious decision to create these protections and elevate them to positions of prominence. You reacted, as we all did, to a barrage of stimuli during childhood and adolescence. Then, your defenses served you in a genuine, yet primitive attempt to fend off attacks on your fledgling self-esteem.

If you were abused during those early years your defensive strategies have become quite powerful and may be more difficult to release. Your personal growth efforts have brought you here and you want to see what will be coming next. You have chosen to move out of chaos and onto the path called Ascension!

Summary of Main Players

Ego: This is the center of the human form which is designed to protect and guide us on our terrestrial journey. For those of you familiar with the Eastern concept of chakras, the ego is associated with the lower three, starting at the root.

Protector-Controller: This is a subset of ego and includes strong protective strategies and rigid postures toward what is often construed as a threatening world.

Observer Self: The part of you that sees what is going on in your life. That part that you consider being "you." This is the part that questions, evaluates and makes decisions about obtaining help for yourself when you realize that you have been engaging in repetitive self-defeating patterns.

Self / Inner Child: This is the feeling aspect of your personality and your true center. The inner child is an early representation of Self, often abandoned because of traumatic experiences. Easily hurt and capable of victim thinking as a result of early traumas, this aspect must be rescued, healed and helped to grow again. To become a mature Self, the inner child needs to be nourished through processes of self-awareness, self-responsibility and self-acceptance.

Angry Self: A component of the inner Child/Self that guards and sometimes lashes out against real or perceived abusers, intruders and similar threats.

Hurt Self: An aspect of the inner child. This part feels the pain associated with real or perceived denigrations, including put downs, criticisms or anything that reinforces a negative self-view. This is the part that needs healing.

Summary of Main Defenses

Projection: Seeing in others what we refuse to accept or view as our own. Usually involves character traits and styles of relating that one denies in oneself and denigrates in others.

Dissociation: Splitting off parts of the Self that have been shamed or abused in a deeply hurtful manner.

Denial: This is an outright rejection of the facts of a situation or behavior that negatively impacts the Self: for example, denial of smoking's true ramifications. Denial can be either a conscious or unconscious process.

Numbing Out: This is characterized by obsessions and compulsions such as substance abuse or other processes that numb unpleasant and unwanted feelings about situations or behaviors that have had negative impact.

Rationalization: This is the process of convincing our Selves and others of stories about why things are the way they are even in the presence of contradictory evidence. This functions to protect a false self-image.

Review

These sub-personalities and defensive strategies are the main characters we deal with in our efforts to cleanse ourselves of emotional wounds related to past injuries and associated thoughts. In so doing, we pave the way for a bright new future that will become our new way of life. We rescue ourselves from various unhealthy defense mechanisms because we want to be free to express who we are at the feeling and Heart level. Our ego and associated defenses move from the foreground of our lives and onto the sidelines where they belong. This allows our Selves to come forward as the new director in our inner world and opens the gateway to the Divine within. We realize we are not only part of God, but that we are God and are able to step onto our proper path.

In order to reach this important turning point, we must precipitate the disintegration of all negative forces related to the ego. These defensive walls must come down because they are non-discriminatory. As much as they may keep potential abusers away, they also keep us apart from our true Selves and all of the associated creativity. We cannot progress until we undertake a revamping of these negative personality structures. Our Selves need to be released so we can fulfill our individual missions.

Example of Journaling

Now that we see the inner workings of our psychological dramas, we can identify and describe our various players and associated defense strategies. We can give them all voices so they will speak to us and show us who they are. This is where our journaling and inner dialogues will take us, to this underworld of unconscious activity where we can meet these players and ultimately make peace with them.

Begin dialoguing with all your players from this point forward. When you feel something stirring inside, ask who wants to speak. Give them a name such as Hurt Self, Angry Self, Scared Self, Protector-Controller or Inner Child. Allow whoever wants to speak to do so. Then you, as Observer Self and moderator, can begin the process of engagement. Here's an example.

Angry Self: "I am so pissed off at you. Why did you do that? Why did you hurt me? Why did you let that person get close to me? Why didn't you see what was coming. I am so pissed at you."

Me: "I can see that you are very angry with me. I can see that you are hurt by my choices. I can see that you want to rage against me right now."

Angry Self: "Yes, you stupid ass, that is exactly so. I hate you! I hate you! I hate you! You are nothing but a jerk and a thorn in my side."

Me: "I hear you. You are very angry with me. Somehow I let you down. You are hurt and you want to lash out at me for what you believe I did wrong."

Note: Never answer this voice's questions or complaints. Only reflect back what you have heard, and that you understand how this part of you feels and how angry it is toward you at this moment. You are talking with a child and that child's feelings need to be validated. If you engage in a debate, then you have lowered yourself to that childish point of view and are now arguing with yourself. Your ego will love this because it keeps you stuck and derails you from the journey you have ventured upon.

Do not edit any of this dialogue as it comes out. This is not about writing a novel. It is about getting the hurt, pain and anger out. Whatever your hurt Self feels, needs to be released, expressed and validated. If your ego or hurt Self wants to call you names, let them do so. This is pure and simple venting, and no one is going to be hurt. That part of you just wants to be heard.

To repeat, we call this venting. Those unknown parts of you will begin venting quite wildly at first because there's a backup in unexpressed anger, hurt and fear. Your job, as with any child, is to listen and reflect back what you have heard. This is how the inner parts of you begin to feel acknowledged. You've had arguments with people where each has lashed out at the other. No one wins and each goes away feeling as angry and upset as when the conflict first erupted. But when someone says "I hear what you're saying," "I understand your frustration," "It must be hard to feel that way," then the anger subsides. At long last someone is finally listening. How else are you going to get to know yourself unless you take the time to listen?

In short order, the tension and energy behind the verbiage will begin to wane. Your hurt and angry Self will tone down the venomous tirade and will allow to you hear what it is feeling. Fear looms behind these conversations. Feelings of fear increase as you probe and question yourself on various beliefs you held and defensive strategies you employed. Whenever you set about to change something within, defenses become rattled and fear raises the emotional temperature.

This primitive structure that you designed for your protection is now feeling threatened. Your ego is not happy to see you breaching the walls. Whenever you attend to something pressing from within, your psychological defenses will step up and try to undermine your efforts by belittling your desire to change and grow. These voices must be heard and acknowledged. It's easy, for example, to let the inner child speak when it is speaking sweetly and behaving like a puppy at the pet store. But when your angry Self steps up, it looks more like the guard dog Cerberus and can be very threatening indeed. We tend to deny and block from awareness those parts simply because they are threatening.

The reason these parts are angry is because they have been disowned. This is where the process begins, with lots of anger and hurt being released. You will have hundreds of these dialogues. Getting acquainted with those disowned parts is a lifelong commitment. But it will not take you a lifetime to move into the open where you can freely and consciously move forward.

When you choose growth over complacency, you choose your Self over the voices of others. When you commit to your ultimate purpose in this life, remarkable changes begin to occur. Your Higher Self will exert increased pressure to resolve internal issues. Your emerging Self will demand more and more of your attention as it begins to trust the process. Each dialogue will take you further into those unconscious regions where your strong and nurturing players are waiting. There will be your creative Self, your dynamic Self, your God Self, your passionate Self, your curious Self, your expressive Self—Your Self! Your Self! Your Self! This will be your connection to the Divine within. You will hear God's voice alongside of your own. The Divine will inform you of your purpose and mission for this lifetime. It will deliver gifts to you in the form of ideas and insights, talents and opportunities with like-minded souls who are also on this same path as you. You are now engaged in the holiest of tasks, actualizing your Self.

Remember, you will encounter resistance as you continue to move forward. This is normal. You will hear from the broader dimensions of yourself and you will hear them often. You are learning to live your life from the inside out now, rather than the ego-centered-outside-in mode that had you trapped until now. This takes time. But with the new energies bombarding Earth and your will to progress, this will take less time than it has taken others, myself included. If you choose to learn your lessons the hard way, it takes longer. You have the benefit of all the decades of my and other inner explorer's experiences laid out before you. Your task is to take advantage of what is offered so you will be better prepared for the work ahead.

Begin your journaling with a simple dialogue that helps you get to know the players within your psyche. Introduce yourself to them as if you were meeting a group of co-workers for the first time. Tell them who you are and what you are about to do. Invite them to participate when they feel up to it. Apologize for not getting there sooner. Inform them that you had other matters to take care of so that you could now make them your priority. Listen to who wants to talk and let them do so. The rest will be watching and listening. The message will go out to all your inner players that you are ready to listen.

When I first began this process, it was chaos. Now I have pet names for all my inner players. At this point they know we are all under new management. The Self is at the helm and we consult with our Higher Power daily for spiritual nourishment and direction. The more we work at this, the clearer the communications become. The Divine is waiting for you within. You will feel and hear the stirrings and will be encouraged to move at your own rhythm and pace. No more guessing! No more wondering! No more blind faith! A direct link to your own power and creativity will be established that is yours alone. Your dynamic Self is waiting. Now is the time!

22 - Making Choices

We assume that making choices is a simple process. We see what's in front of us and we choose the best option. That's the way it goes in an ideal choice-making process. But what if it were not that simple? Let's face it; people make the wrong choices every day. The wrong girlfriend! The wrong boyfriend! The wrong destination! The wrong job and so on. Choice-making is not as simple as it may seem. Smokers continue to smoke. Drinkers continue to drink. Drug users continue to use. If making good choices were so simple, then the above situations would not exist.

Look at your own life for a moment.

Have all your choices been wise ones? Is there a repeating pattern of choices occurring that continues to produce the same negative result? Why are you still making it? When it comes to life choices, we can see that this process is not as simple as choosing the right candy, or movie, or other form of entertainment.

True free choice is based on personal characteristics, prehistory and awareness. How aware you are of your prehistory determines why you are making the same faulty decisions over and over again. Why does a woman continue to choose abusive men? Why does a man continually succumb to the definitions and desires of perceived authority figures? While it appears in such examples that there is no choice, only repeating patterns, the fact is there is choice. Not choosing, as a default position, is still a choice.

Choice-making still occurs, even outside our conscious awareness. A part of us makes choices based on prehistory, old patterns and familiar expectations. For example, the assertion that you never get what you want is more a belief based on prehistory. You may continue to recreate a situation where you feel deprived, but at some level this is a choice. You can alter any outcome by making a different and yes, a conscious choice.

As children, we react to our environment. You adopt the status quo; that is, how things work in your family of origin. We make unconscious choices based on survival value. If a parent always yells at a child when it needs something, then the child determines that it doesn't need, or that its needs can only be met indirectly through some form of manipulation.

In so doing, the child relinquishes the conscious desire to have the need met! You can see that after a few dozen times of having needs neither validated nor met that the child just gives up trying. And worse, the child convinces him or herself that needs are not worth pursuing or that there is no need at all. An unhealthy and dysfunctional family typically promotes reactive and unconscious choices. This is the root of negative choices.

Very few people would consciously choose a situation or pattern with a guaranteed negative outcome. When people call upon common sense as the platform for making informed choices, they are simply quoting their own point of view. Individuals making negative choices are quite aware of common sense; they just don't see the repeating pattern until it is pointed out to them. The fact that so many choices are made at unconscious levels cancels out the notion that common sense is the basis for all decision making. Patterns return because they are familiar and familiarity seems safer. Making new and healthier choices occurs when an individual is prepared to examine their negative repeating patterns.

Making a choice for a healthy life often precipitates a crisis, certainly for the part of you that makes unconscious choices. We have referred to this part of your defenses as the protector-controller. This part of you has a big investment in maintaining control. For example, you might numb out when an important critical choice has to be made. But you are still making a choice; only you are choosing not to choose. The necessary decision-making process is relegated to your unconscious which relies on established patterns. How many times have you asked yourself why you keep doing the same thing over and over resulting in the same undesirable outcome? When you allow this unconscious protector-controller aspect to make the choice, you can see the now familiar negative result. This once again confirms that you are the victim of forces beyond your control.

What has to happen on a conscious level for this pattern to change?

The answer is key: "Know Thyself." This is no small order. No matter who you are, even well-trained psychologists, therapists and counselors can have troubling unconscious messages to confront. It is crucial that you get to the bottom of it. You have to see that those unconscious choices exist and that they do not work to your benefit. What once had survival value during childhood is now a detriment to your healthy development as an evolving and productive adult.

All of us have had occasion to witness some adult friend behaving like a child, or to recognize that occasionally we have felt like a child in need of a mother's comfort. These are common enough experiences to which we can all relate. The primary sign of true adult development is emotional maturity. This includes the ability to make choices based on the evidence at hand and not the programming from one's past. True freedom comes when our hurtful past is laid to rest. It doesn't mean we have forgotten the pain, it means we do not let that pain control our lives and decisions anymore.

This freedom comes when we take hold of ourselves and declare: "I am now making the decisions, not my protector-controller, not my abused and frightened Self, not my victim Self, or any part of me that came into being before I could make conscious choices. My choices will henceforth be conscious choices." When we create a safer and healthier environment for ourselves, we can mature emotionally and become better capable of making informed choices. We can provide ourselves with healthy parenting and be free to be our Selves.

In unhealthy dysfunctional environments, conscious choice-making is most often absent. We react. We resist. We counterattack. We may become passive-aggressive, resisting pressure through subtle non-compliance. We identify ourselves as victims because we feel victimized. And we make limited, uninformed choices based on those early stressful circumstances.

In these stressful environments, there is no such thing as free choice. Survival is paramount. "What do I need do to survive this stress?" replaces "What choice would I like to make at this time?" We come to believe that we are what is happening to us; we are the victim, the abused, the abandoned, and so on. Name your injured identity.

How do you change your reactive choice to conscious choice?

You become aware of whom you are at this point in time, and aware of what happened to you when those earlier unconscious choices were made. Only then can you determine what you need to change in order to grow. You make a conscious choice to better your life. You seek resources that will help you untie all your psychological and emotional knots. You choose to open yourself up to the inner you, the person you are inside, unencumbered by shame or emotional injury.

You choose to get in touch with your full potential and to clean out all the garbage, negative messages and pain that you have held onto. You are choosing your freedom. This is what is meant by Conscious Evolution. Now you know you have a choice. You can continue to live out your life in a pattern of prepackaged reactions that were shaped and triggered by others, or, you can live your life consciously and happily, as it was meant to be lived.

I made this commitment 40 years ago and still work at it. It's not as difficult anymore, and I've had fun along the way. I have actually enjoyed untangling many of the psychological knots that were part of my prehistory. What I needed came along in one form or another – a good counselor, a friend, many great books, an inspiring movie, and so on. As I learned to take responsibility for my feelings, my life improved. I improved. I became stronger. I benefited from every one of my conscious choices and took the remedial steps required to heal past injuries as I became aware of them.

As I learned to overcome defeat and curtail negative self-references, I gained confidence and positive self-esteem. As I realized that a part of me (protector-controller) seemed programmed to hold me back, be reactive and undermine me, I took away its power and claimed it for myself.

This is The Hero's Journey from Mythology.
To our inner world we must travel, to confront the defenses put up by our protector-controller, to engage these and overcome them so we can recover our essential Selves. We do this for one simple reason, to become all that we can be and live the life we were meant to have. This can be a long and difficult journey at times, but I've never met anyone who said it wasn't worth it. I wouldn't trade my journey for any other experience. That's the level of my commitment and the joy of the rewards that come with it.

Whatever it takes of me, wherever I need to go, I will do it. I am worth it, and so are you! Commit to the full expression of your being and watch your life take a turn for the better.

23 - The Dialogues

You may think this process may be challenging or, perhaps even a bit scary. In fact, it is both. Decide that you are worth it and give it a try. I've been involved in this process for over 40 years and I can assure you it works. This process may also sound difficult, awkward or even weird, but I encourage you to give it your best effort. It holds much potential for personal growth. If you are willing to set aside a little embarrassment and feelings of awkwardness, you will learn valuable information about your Self. Through this process you will grow, and develop skills and understandings about yourself and your place in the world that you could not have imagined.

Begin by taking a deep breath and announcing (out loud) to the world that you are going to begin talking with yourself. Say it: "World, I am now going to begin talking with myself and I don't care what you think!" Say it three times. Feel it and believe it as you say it.

Who speaks up first? Is it your ego or the protector-controller? Is it your wounded and hurting inner child? Or is it your Self that wants to be connected to Soul? The responses coming from each may be somewhat different, but they will give you a glimpse as to what's going on with you at this time. Here is a sample of some typical responses.

Your protector-controller and your ego will likely tell you that you are crazy or stupid or some other demeaning judgment. These parts of you may also tell you that the author of these ideas and this book does not know of what he speaks. If you acquiesce to these notions, then that would be the end of it, and this book would be closed. The process of your personal emancipation would end post haste.

This is where you step forth and declare your intentions to further this journey. When you believe that you can enter into a dialogue with different parts of yourself, the protector-controller and ego will offer the same condemnation that this is a crazy venture: "Why would you do this? Who do you think you are? Are you crazy?" These are typical autocratic responses coming from the various frightened parts within you.

These frightened and condemning voices surface because when you journal, they have no control over the outcome. By issuing forth judgments, they seek to intimidate you to the point where you react unwittingly and slam the door on this line of inquiry. This is the kind of reasoning that tends to come up in a conflict between you and you. You might feel silly and awkward at first. Dialoguing with yourself might seem foolish, self-aggrandizing or narcissistic, but when your answers take you deeper into your inner world, then you've won valuable insights and expanded your self-understanding. If your inquiry convinces you that this process is ludicrous, then your protector-controller and ego have prevailed. Aside from feeling a bit awkward at first, you have nothing to lose when you try.

Begin this process by asking your protector-controller or ego why they want to avoid this line of inquiry. Let them speak to you on the pages of your journal. Let them say what they want to say. As you listen and write down their responses, be sure to pay attention to the fear behind their objections. In fact, call them on it. "I hear that you are fearful and I want you to tell me about that." Let them talk about that fear and record it on the page.

Whatever they offer you becomes an avenue for further investigation. You will begin to learn about whom they are and how they perceive themselves within your personal psychodynamics. Remember, they have roles to play and a protective vigilance to maintain in case you wander off the prescribed path. Their admonitions are simply a reflection of your indoctrinations. Their job is to bring you back to "normal" as defined by your cultural and personal experiences and the current status quo. They have a large investment in maintaining a ritualized approach to life. Their objective is to keep fear at bay by - you guessed it – keeping you afraid of looking inward.

Now, dialogue with your Protector-Controller to understand its perspective and role in your life!

Getting to know your Fearful Self!

Pay attention to the objections coming from your protector-controller. This part of you will react strongly to any line of questioning because one of its key jobs has been to protect you from the discomforting fear that you are actually experiencing. Remember, you are simply conducting an investigation. You want to know more about your inner life, about how things work inside, and about all the different functions that occur below conscious awareness.

This is part of your heroic journey. The journey includes investigation, probing, inquiry and ultimately, full disclosure and self-discovery. The journey culminates in the meeting and confrontation of all your inner players, regardless of how frightening these encounters may appear to be. This is heroism par excellence, the willingness to transcend your fear and go where so few people go, the willingness to see and assess for yourself all of the inner dynamics that have been pulling you away from your Self. This takes courage and that's why human history has dubbed this process as heroic.

The hero's journey will take you to the "heart of the beast." If you are frightened at this prospect, then it is time to have a dialogue with your frightened Self and to determine what it wants and what it fears. After the dialogue, report back to where you left off here.

Dialogue with your Fearful Self

You've had a lively discussion with an important aspect of your Self, the scared and frightened part. How is that part of you doing? Is it really that scared? Or, did that part of you just want your attention for a while?

Are you beginning to understand that these parts of you want your notice? They don't want to be denied or rejected. They want to be part of the fabric of your existence. They want to be with you. They could continue to get by without your participation and acknowledgement of them because they have done so for years. But this is not what they truly want. They yearn for you to take them under your wing, embrace them and come to know them. All the energy that you utilized and lost to avoid feeling and understanding these aspects of Self can be reclaimed. With fear and rejection being owned and acknowledged, that formerly wasted energy will now be at your disposal to create a more productive and peaceful life.

Become One with Your Self and you will become One with God.

Pause and reflect once again.

I am steering you toward yourself, and not some external entity. I am steering you toward your inner Self. I am urging you to move closer to that which lies within, and that which is yours and yours alone. Discern for yourself as you work through these processes. Pause and reflect. Ask yourself if this makes sense to you. Listen to your Heart and its response. What do you feel? What do you hear? What makes sense to you?

Why am I pointing you toward your Self?

The dialogues that you have with your various component selves all lead to somewhere very important. They will take you to your Heart. Your Heart, being connected to your Soul, receives information from your earth plane experiences that it uploads to your Soul. Your Soul absorbs, translates and then transfers this data back to Source which revels in your new learning. As a Divine being, you and I learn about life and grow on the earth plane by walking in this world of materiality. Source is always eager to grow and expand. As representatives of the Source you and I are endowed with that desire as well.

There is only one ultimate purpose in this world, and that is to grow. That is what the Divine wants for all of us, and for Itself. Everything we achieve enriches the Divine. Life on the material plane is a growth experience if we so choose and those experiences enhance All-That-Is, including our Selves being at one with the Divine.

Are you ready to grow? Are you ready to learn all you can about who and what you are? Then let's move on.

Our Approach

Our approach is certainly not about bringing Eastern practices to a Western style of life. It is not about upholding some long standing status quo that's brought us war, poverty and similar forms of grief. It is about bringing the inside out, by reactivating mythology and integrating it with modern psychology. In fact, modern psychology is derived from mythology. It relies on many symbols of myth to make its case about the different dimensions of our interior life.

Modern psychology has attempted to bring the scientific method into its approach so it could justify itself in the current academic and medical communities. This approach has met with limited success and resulted in the amputation of many realms of experience that do not lend themselves to simple numeric values. A qualitative approach is a more valid method to explore the meanings and themes lying behind human experiences. When we ask about our anxiety, for example, we do not ask for a quantitative analysis. We want a description that we can relate to.

Mythology is not a scientific line of inquiry. It provides simple descriptive stories that help elucidate important points about life and personal growth. Mythology was once considered a form of magic through storytelling. It was never intended to be science in the strictest sense of measurement, analysis and outcome. But it has proven to be science in the sense of non-quantitative forms of reliability and validity. The themes of mythology recur with predictable regularity. Myths have been mapped and collated by investigators like Joseph Campbell. He demonstrated the universality of myth and its application across cultures and throughout the passage of time with countless generations relying upon it.

Mythology today still stands tall despite its denigration as synonymous with falsehood. Mythology has been with us since the dawn of time and has brought us understandings that you and I consider valuable to this very day. Why else would we keep repeating mythological themes in our movies and television programs? Every day we are served another buffet of mythical imagery and lessons to be learned. Psychology uses the stories of mythology to regularly explain human behavior, life, attitudes and important lessons. Mythology correlates with our map of our psychological world, our inner dynamics and our communications with Self and ego.

Man is a mythmaker. And man survives through those myths. They guide and teach succeeding generations on the basic principles of life. The ultimate goal of myth is to lead us back to our Source and our understanding of our personal power as it resonates with our Divinity.

The Dialogues Continued

To this point we have had conversations with our protector-controller and ego. We have spoken directly with our frightened Self and a host of other feelings. It is time to ask what else within us needs to be given attention and spoken with.

Angry Self: This part of us has been hiding inside waiting for a chance to speak out. If you are not aware of any unexpressed anger within, that's fine. Simply ask if there is any anger that wants to speak to you and express your willingness to listen and respond. For some, anger has been hiding behind the scenes for a long time. In some cases, anger has been playing hide and seek with us since we first became aware of our place in the world. Anger can be both our strength when we assert ourselves or our weakness when we try and stuff it down. Healthy anger literally shakes things up and tells us when we've been violated. Repressed anger turns into rage and comes out as abuse toward others or ourselves. Your anger has a lot to say about what's going on in your life. Talk to your anger now.

Take out your journals and begin to dialogue with your anger.

Your protector-controller won't like this conversation and may want to interfere. Let it briefly state its case in one sentence or less. Then tell the protector-controller that you will speak with it later. For the time being, you are addressing your angry Self and this is your focus.

Begin. Ask the anger who it is and what role it plays in your life. Remember to reflect back what you hear. Remember to pass no judgments. Do not be argumentative. Your sole goal at this time is to explore for the purpose of gaining insight. Your angry Self will have a lot to say about many subjects. Today is a get-to-know-you session. Your anger is about to declare itself to you because you have given permission for it to speak and be heard. Your other players are watching when you dialogue. They know what is going on and have a hint as what to expect.

Dialogue with your Angry Self

This dialoguing process is not frivolous, but it can be fun. Getting to know your Self is one of the greatest joys in life. Remember all the things you discovered when you were a child . . . butterflies, tall grass, trees to climb, crawling insects, babies gurgling, adults dancing, music, mud, water, birds, dogs, cats, different colored humans. Now you're getting to know yourself and all the internal players that make up your life. These are the same players we have identified in mythology.

We became dissociated from our inner world long ago. We projected different parts of ourselves over the globe, and then we went looking for them. We are the wandering tribes, the prodigal sons and daughters, and the adventurers seeking new landscapes, new challenges and new knowledge. And we are the heroes and heroines looking for lost and discarded parts of ourselves.

We are explorers of a different kind. We have recently focused our curiosity and efforts inward with an aim of finding our way Home. This is the "return" portion of our mighty adventure, just as it has been described in myth. Apparently, we have split off parts of ourselves before, in previous lives, and then recovered them to our great delight. We are now reassembling the final pieces of this patchwork called Self. We need to be whole for the next step in our Conscious Evolution. We seek to reconnect and re-own those deepest parts of ourselves that we abandoned during our quest for glory and wealth in the material world.

We have recently witnessed the collapse of giant financial institutions that were based on the premise that "more is better." We have seen powerful business figures being trotted off to jail. These very same people asserted repeatedly that the free market is the best way to do business and then we watched as these same banking and insurance managers held out their hands for rescue money from taxpayers. Many of us are now victims of these financial fiascos. This is the consequence when egos are in charge and no longer connected to the Heart. This is what happens when winning at any cost is the end game, no matter whose investments or livelihoods are destroyed.

Getting to know yourself from the inside out will keep you out of harm's way. As you learn to trust yourself, through your continued use of self-dialogue, you will see the world in a vastly different way. You will value your own opinion first, and have the capacity to see through the many distractions and half-truths that are constantly delivered by governments and large institutions. Getting to know yourself is your best answer for a healthy and prosperous life.

Summary

We are learning that we are multidimensional entities by engaging in an examination of the breadth of our inner experience. Our inner life is rich with surprises. We must open our hearts and minds and continue digging deeper to uncover these surprises. Then we can make them our own.

We've been talking about Ascension since the beginning of Part II. We can see that our prelude, the mythical journey of the hero, stands as a roadmap to our newly revealed discoveries. We have been looking inside for the past few decades because we are being drawn back to our point of origin. We originated from the Divine, and our journey will return us to that place called "home" from whence we came. We are now completing the intermediate portion of our journey, the part which is referred to as "initiation" in mythology.

The "return" portion of the heroic journey is demanding, but uplifting. Many heroes and heroines experience a new-found happiness. Humility, rather than bravado, is now our best calling card because egos have no place in our relationship with Source. Our desire is to ascend and lead the way for others. We will become The Army of Light.

Light is the essence of the Divine. It is our essence as well. Clearing out the encumbrances that blocked our inner light has been our main mission at this time. We are reuniting with our Loved One, our Central Self, our Soul and our Source. We are coming Home.

We are, after all, feeling, sentient beings that are well aware of that which surrounds us. Our essential Self has been crippled by years of unhealthy subjugation by others, such as religious and educational institutions, and, ultimately, by our own behavior. We learned to employ a variety of defense mechanisms in order to feel safe. It is time to realize that we are already good enough at the Heart and feeling level, so we can let go of those influences that have held us back.

Continue your dialogues with all parts of you. Through these efforts you will make peace with yourself. Get to know the different players who make up your inner world and bring them home through your dialogues and self-acceptance. Love yourself as you would have others love you.

Love others as you would like to be loved. Love your God Self because that is who you are.

Transformation

When I feel emotionally crushed, I feel it psychologically and spiritually as well. Every part of me feels shattered, broken and bleeding in every sense except the physical.

My body remains intact, but the psychological structures that support it are in disarray. This is the essence of emotional disintegration at the cellular level. I have been through this on a number of occasions during the course of my growth journey. Each time I come back together at a healthier and stronger level.

It is difficult to go through a process such as this. It is a shattering experience. Everything you've relied on feels broken and strewn across the floor of your life. Your old ideas, your old dreams, your old hopes are all shattered. They need to be replaced.

There is a temptation to pick up those pieces and attempt a reintegration, but going back to the old way is no longer possible. Only a new structure can replace this mess. When you feel shattered, broken and bleeding, there's nothing much to do but wait. In no time, some part of you will begin speaking and show you another way to grow.

That's just part of the reconstruction process. The old has to break down before the new can begin to emerge. Your body, mind and spirit will come back together as a new and stronger you. Accept the feelings of anxiety but try not to dwell on them, as they will pass too.

You are letting go of something you don't need any more, like a snake shedding its old skin. The snake no longer needs that skin because a new one has been growing underneath. The spiritual and emotional growth you've been practicing has taken shape underneath and is ready to surface. A newer, fresher version of who you are is coming to the fore.

You will feel vulnerable for a while, naked in the storm of life some might say. That old skin kept you comfortable with its familiarity and predictability. As with all things in nature, a new order wants to be established and the old has to make room for the new.

Like the snake, we crawl into the deep grass with our anxiety and fear and wait for that old skin to come off. Once that is accomplished, we may need to stay for a while because we will feel vulnerable. That's okay. Take all the time you need. You will be ready to move forward soon enough. This is the nature of transformation.

A certain point is reached where the old order crumbles to make room for the new. This is called Positive Disintegration. This is the hope for our future as human beings. Many people want to hang on at this point, fearing the disappearance of the familiar. But our deeper nature has an agenda too, and pushing you to grow beyond current limits is an important aspect which motivates and offers encouragement. It's easy to surrender once you become aware of what's going on inside.

The direction we take after the transformation depends on what we have been building underneath. Some of you have been using positive affirmations. Others have been engaged in spiritual writing and growth workshops. These early efforts, along with the dialogues recommended here, will bring you to the next step. You know when it's time to restart growth process. There will be something new knocking at your door that wants to be brought into conscious awareness and you will feel compelled to open that door.

There is really no going back to the old status quo. No matter how much you may want to or how hard you try, you cannot unlearn what you've been learning. You realize that a part of you is very excited and hopeful about this new found awareness and growth.

What you're feeling is the excitement children feel with every new step they take. Each step changes the way you relate to yourself and the world around you. This new self-order is demonstrated by those things you've been working toward, and a few surprises as well. We don't fully know what we're building underneath until it comes out to greet us. That's the surprise and the joy of creation.

Where do we go from here with this emerging Self, this new being arising from within? We've been developing this by taking courses, reading books, doing exercises, changing our rhythm and vibration, exploring new worlds and opening ourselves to ever expanding possibilities. The Creative Force has been at work with our active participation. Your Higher Self has been active behind the scenes all along, pushing and prodding, urging you to take chances and try something different. Slowly but surely you open to that center where your inner guidance lives and you make the connection.

This is no mere fancy. This is not about faith. This is simple and palpable experience that you recognize as your own. Your Higher Self, your Soul, is your director and you recognize that part of you because it is You. You and I are simply an incarnate version of Source's curiosity, love and joy.

We are designed to grow through self-responsibility. Our human nature is programmed for growth. Our spiritual nature desires to grow. Only growth matters in the grand scheme. Source seeks to grow and mature. We, as sparks from the Divine, can grow along with Source, if we so choose.

God's urging for us to shed our old skin arrives in a timely fashion. It is the correct course for this moment in our evolution. Such events are rarely convenient, but they are necessary. Let yourself shed that old skin now. A transformation is upon you. You may feel shattered, broken and, perhaps, disillusioned for a while, but that will soon pass. You have been renewed and are set to emerge. Let that be your gift to yourself and to Source. It's time to show the world your shiny new Self.

24 – Destination Ascension

We've seen the brochures. We're excited about our final destination. Our main goal for this venture is full conscious awareness. We are on the upward climb of the mountain called Ascension. We have set up a base camp we call Integration. We have been speaking with different parts of ourselves to bring them onboard as we set our sights for the summit. We will be talking with our players again and again as we set off for this final trek.

Your kit bags are full of all the tools you need.

<u>Flexibility:</u> This is the ability to move with the times. Whatever comes at you, move with it. No more resistance even in the face of so-called impossible odds. You can maneuver around and through all obstacles as they present themselves, knowing they are there to strengthen you.

<u>Love:</u> This is the singular guiding beacon of Ascension. Ascension is about falling in love with our truest Selves. Making peace with your players allows you to bring the whole family along, even those parts that are kicking and screaming in protest. Treat these like children who don't know yet that they are going to have a good time. Talk to them. Cajole them. Reassure them. But let them know in no uncertain terms this is the way you are headed.

<u>Inner Guidance:</u> Inner guidance comes through the heart center. Your Higher Self, speaking to you through your heart, reminds you of your true purpose in this life. Through this channel, you will be reminded of the contract you agreed to prior to this incarnation.

All heroes and heroines make contracts with themselves and their inner guidance in order to remain true to their purposes. What's the point of trekking if you change your mind half way through your journey? That is not commitment. Sticking with the familiar seems easier. No one can do your ascension and personal growth for you. Heroines and heroes follow their hearts, walk their own path and check in with Source regularly to make sure they have not strayed from their path.

Going for the Summit

Now, we are headed for the summit. It is the only destination. We have had many side trips that have taken us off course. We've been down many blind alleys, only to be coaxed back onto our main path.

We agree that our ego doesn't know where it is going. Every time we followed ego's urgings we hit another wall. We are done with that. Our Self is the only guidance worthy of consideration. This part knows exactly where to go because it is informed by God. Our God Self, our Higher Self, knows better than anybody where we need to be. Our wanderings were mere detours which have led us back to destiny's straight and narrow. We simply do not need those ego side trips anymore. We know they lead nowhere.

Our kit bags are full of other resources and valuable supplies such as humility, openness, receptivity, commitment and passion. We realize that humility is a larger blessing than holding onto resentments and hurts that knocked us off the path. Our ego has given way to Self, recognizing that it was totally unprepared where Ascension is concerned. Our inner child is bravely stepping up with its gifts of honesty, creativity and unconditional love.

Our inner child is a master player, leading the orchestra of sub-players toward a healthier destination than any of us could conceive. It always wanted to conduct the orchestra, but was pinned down by the ego's fear mongering. The inner child is now free to be authentically expressive. These expressions will guide us on our journey through Ascension.

You will know that you are ascending because the experience feels expansive, exciting and uplifting. Our hearts are happily dancing to the beat of our own drum, much like those characters skipping along the Yellow Brick Road. The Wizard of Oz is not our destination, because he turned out to be a scam. The real wizard is our Higher Self, hidden behind a curtain that we are now pulling back.

Our story is about heroism and our journey is toward wholeness. As we undertake our preparations and align ourselves with our personal growth, we declare our commitment to The Path of the Hero.

We are now fully engaged in our own process. No distractions and no more side trips. Our goal is that precious gift within. Our Higher Self has been waiting for us there, candle burning brightly, warm fire in the fireplace, cozy blankets to snuggle under and a plethora of other gifts ready to be unwrapped. We are excited. We feel alive. We are open to the possibility of falling in love with ourselves, our lives and all the challenges we've had to face. The reward is feeling "at home" with ourselves, comfortable in our own skins, and finally at peace.

This is what awaits us as we enter the 5th dimension of our lives. All the comforts we once believed were only available to others are there for the taking. Everything your heart desired is waiting for you.

Was it worth it?

To climb out of the morass of conflicted living is the final step toward Ascension. This requires total and complete cleansing of our Soul and Heart center as these are the instruments of our emancipation. Your Heart becomes clear and loving. Your Soul is awakened and speaking through your Heart. Kindness and gentleness, toward yourself and others, feel normal to you now. Ascension is a reality that is completely attainable.

We've reached the pinnacle of human existence for this incarnation. We have surrendered ourselves to Source. We remember that God created us and we are part of God. This knowledge provides us with strength. Rest! Close your eyes and let your connection to God be the conduit of the Divine's boundless love. Feel it. Allow it to flow through you and around you. This love will embrace you and free you of any final encumbrances.

Ascension, you now know, has been completely attainable. It tempted you. It invited you. It cajoled you into action. Now it is prepared to teach you. Humility and gratitude are the feelings that announce the summit has been taken. Your Higher Self has served you well, and so has your passion and purpose. You walk around and drink it all in. It's time to celebrate.

You cannot lie to yourself anymore, and why would you? Your life purpose is at hand. Your contract has been completed. You are free to go about your day in the glory of this 5th dimension.   Welcome Home!

25 - Getting the Juices Flowing

When you reach inside yourself, do you find a storehouse of creativity? Or do you feel your creativity has gone AWOL, and you can't find it anywhere? Sometimes we feel we've lost it because it has been overwhelmed by the many distractions in our life.

It can be a long road to travel, trying to return to that creative place. There are obstacles along the way, early life traumas, feelings of hurt, lost loved ones, grievances, upsets and old conflicts brewing in the background. All of these are distractions to the creative elements within.

Children are inherently creative and expressive. They scribble, they write, they color, they take things apart, they sing and dance. They are already there, in that internal world, where the creative mind is at play. And they play, because that's how they create. Their imagination takes them anywhere they desire to go. They don't judge their enthusiastic quests. They just do. This is the essence of creativity – exploring, playing and experimenting with new ideas. This is also the essence of our Inner Child, our creative Self.

Contrast that with adult concerns such as bills to pay, children to feed, dealing with an unfair employer, upheaval in the political world. The list can seem endless. When consumed by all these worries, they become distractions that provide neither time nor energy to be creative.

Lack of creativity is not so much an absence of ability as it is about so many distractions. Solitude is essential for creativity. Watch young children at play. They are happily engaged in their own world and loving every minute of it. Sooner or later, they will come out and show you what they've done. You will applaud. They will go off and do more.

That's what you need, some applause to get you going. Applaud yourself when you bake a cake, build a birdhouse or find a creative solution to financial woes. Creativity may grow in the dark, but requires the spark of light and encouragement to keep it going. As adults, we appreciate being noticed, but it seems harder for us to accept praise. Try receiving for a change. Say thank you when you're complimented and appreciate others for their kind gestures. It validates you as both a giver and receiver of the love embodied in those gestures.

So where's your spark right now? It is there waiting for you, down in that private chamber where you once created as a child. You will recover that for yourself now that you want to retrieve your inner child. You can retrieve that misplaced part and fan that old ember of creativity into a full blown flame.

How do you get there? Cleanse yourself, is the answer. You start journaling as has already been established and demonstrated for you here. Recall that journaling is not creative writing, but writing for the purpose of cleaning out those distractions that reside in your subconscious. You write about every challenge that jumps onto your path. You write about the children, your spouse, the family, your job and your church. You write about your feelings of anger, hurt, betrayal, insecurity and fear, whatever is bothering you. This is journaling for a purpose. And that purpose is cleansing the Soul. A clean slate is the basic creative stance. It means you are ready to begin creating again.

This cleansing process is an ongoing and life-long process. There is always more to clean out. It's a very soothing and satisfying process. You identify and release all those fears, worries and injunctions. Then your creativity flows again. A little bit here, a little bit there, and pretty soon you're filling canvasses with images, cupboards with crafts, workshops with structures and empty pages with stories. You are finding creative solutions to problems you thought could not be solved. You are flowing with your inspiration and going wherever it takes you.

Cleansing via journaling is an emotional and spiritual enema. You get those nasty clogs out of the way and then you start creating again, just as you did in childhood. Our spiritual and emotional selves need regular care just as our physical body does. We need to keep all these systems running smoothly. Creativity is a process; it works best when you get the distractions out of the way, especially old hurts and resentments. Then you can easily do what you came here for – Create! Your Inner Child will love you for it.

26 – Getting Connected

We reviewed much material in our journey through the myths of time. We have seen ourselves hunkered down in defense of our fragile selves only to have them emerge intact at the invitation of our conscious selves. We have traveled up and down many blind alleys to seek answers to our many questions about life and our spiritual purpose.

We are on a journey that we orchestrated with our Divine partner. We are at the point where all these elements will come together in a singular whole. We have sought out mysteries and secrets hidden within. We have entertained ourselves with glimpses of the past and images of an unknown future. We have tirelessly assembled all the tools necessary for our return to our Self, the God within.

We sang and danced and cried out the hurt of our wounds. We are at the point of Ascension of releasing ourselves from greed and subordination, domination and slavery, revenge and loss, hunger and denial, through the conscious re-opening of our fragile hearts.

We are at the point where these delays are behind us. We are summitting to that highest peak that represents our greatest achievement. We are reconnecting to God and consciously activating that Life Force within. We have one final step, and that is our conscious reconnection to Source. After all our trials and tribulations, our sentencing to seemingly endless rounds of therapy, ridding ourselves of boxes and boxes of pain garnered from our current and previous lives, we are ready to surrender to All-That-Is.

This is our ultimate mission. We have come this far and we are not about to stay on the sidelines for this final step. The characters in *The Voice – A Mythological Guide to Mankind's Ascension* showed us that true connection is possible. Feeling and hearing God's Voice inside is within our grasp.

This connection is completely available to us as a matter of course. Our efforts have led us here.

We have completed endless hours of preparation. We have wandered about and bumped into every obstacle imaginable. We have one step left to take and that requires us to cross that Bridge to Hope.

This bridge seems invisible to us at times. When we're not ready to cross this bridge, it's a challenge we cannot overcome; and, sometimes, we are unable to see the bridge. We must be ready. We must have completed all due diligence and left no stone unturned in the re-making of our being. We have come to terms with ego and all its defense mechanisms and distractions. We have committed to being totally honest with ourselves and have enjoyed the benefits of this mode of self-relating. We learn that being truthful means we are no longer vulnerable. It means we are at peace with who we are. Our reward now awaits us.

We've had glimpses into our future with the Oneness of Life. Our God Self has awakened and informed us in many subtle ways about our life and purpose. We have come to terms with the truth of our inner dynamics. We are God incarnate having an adventure on this plane called Earth.

We have sensed that God has been leading us and prodding us along. We have seen the little miracles that have been delivered to us. We have experienced for ourselves the truth behind the Hero Myth and its simple straightforward guidance for multiple generations of humans. We have placed ourselves on that very path and adopted the strategies that previous heroes and heroines have engaged with success.

We are now well aware of our futures and destinies in time. We have glimpsed the future and chosen to join. We are ready to embrace the bliss of becoming our Christ Self. There is a second coming and it is here. We are the second coming of Christ as that energy emerges through our hearts. We are the Divine's representatives on Earth known as The Army of Light. Now we can directly communicate with this part of us.

Journal Exercise

Take out your journals and start a dialogue with your God Self, your inner Divinity, your Christ nature, whatever name you wish to ascribe to it. That part of you awaits your first direct communication, as has been hinted at for weeks and months now, if not years. Your Divine Nature is ready for you.

Prepare to be astonished! Prepare to feel some trepidation! Prepare to hear from your ego that you are going mad! You've heard those counter arguments in our previous sections as you dialogued with different parts of yourself. Ask yourself: "How can I be mad as I sit here listening to my God Self provide instructions and guidance about my life?"

Choose! The time is at hand. You have gained so much through your recovery and healing. Your therapy brought you answers that you didn't have before. The miracle you were hoping for has arrived. You are that miracle. You and your conscious choice to grow have delivered the substance of your recovery and impending Ascension. Congratulations!

As you engage in conversation with your Higher Self, begin to ask the questions about which you have wondered. Feel or sense those answers and write them down. Let your pen glide across the page guided by source and that energetic feeling that has wrapped itself around you. Can you feel that feeling of heightened energy buzzing around your body? Heightened energy means heightened awareness. Attentiveness! Alertness!

Allow yourself to feel awkward, if that is the case, as your ego protests. Write what you feel, hear, sense or see. Write it all down. It is yours to have and to hold and to later reflect upon.

At first Source will seem very far away, like some alien entity. Twenty-five years ago we were reading about Ramtha, Seth and similar disembodied messengers who came to us through willing vehicles just like ourselves. It took a while to trust them. We had to parcel out the medium from the message in order to appreciate that the message made sense. When I first recognized that I might channel, I could not believe it. I had previously made some contact but never believed it was to a higher part of me. I wanted my own Ramtha to come through so that I could be unique, powerful and popular. That was my ego, of course, more than willing to adopt that pose if it led to some kind of glory and recognition.

Not anymore! What I hear and feel is mine from my Higher Self and Divine Source. My ego has no say in any of it. These are the only true entities in my inner environment. Together we are One. The more I surrender, the more closely I am in touch. Now, connecting is a regular event for me, like sitting down to write this book. Almost daily, I have conversations with my Higher Self.

Are you ready for your connection? Your God Self is waiting. You're the one who has to reach out. You're the one who has to trust. All your prayers, affirmations and spiritual counseling sessions have been about self-trust. Here it is. This is your time to shine. You can reclaim that natural ability to trust and connect with your Divine nature. How does that feel?

Does this idea frighten you? Have you jumped back in retreat? Have you seen the mountaintop and turned away, feeling unworthy? Did you believe this program was just another set of exercises designed to move you an inch or two along your path? Here's the truth in a nutshell.

You have arrived! You are ready to converse with your Higher Self! He/She is waiting for you! Now is the time! Go to your journal and have a dialogue with your Higher Self.

You have begun what will be a lifelong conversation with your Higher Self. Each time you do so, you will be open to more of that Divine energy. Soon you will be completely immersed in it, as part of the ascension experience. This is the goal of this book, to help you connect with Source.

You are here now and you've had your first meaningful conversation with the Divine within you. How do you feel? Was it too easy? Are you speechless? Is your ego going mad? Well, get used to it. You are now connecting with God. God will steer you from here on, unless, of course, you choose to return to ego captivity, which is highly unlikely.

Take a deep breath and enter a world of beauty, excitement and growth affirming challenge. There are no boundaries here except those you might erect.

It can feel overwhelming to stand your own ground, inside the truth of your being. You will probably feel wobbly for a time, like that child you once were when you were learning to walk. Stand up. Fall down. Stand up. Walk a bit. Fall down. So it goes with anything new. You're learning to trust the truest part of your being. That flies in the face of everything you've been taught about goals and precision and linear crossings of unfathomable depths. You are now the Hero and Heroine of your journey. You have stepped onto the Bridge to Hope and crossed that void from ego-centeredness to spiritually-centered connection and guidance. You are rid of all identifiable obstacles and have surrounded yourself with the gifts of the Universe. Be pleased with your achievement!

"Prepare to take your leave," you may now say to ego. "Your role as leader is done. I am walking with my Higher Self now. This will be my Light and Source. It is my Divine inheritance. It is my inner truth. It knows better than anyone where I need to go."

Your ego can continue to be in charge of your lower chakras, those that connect you to the Earth. But your new foundation, your new root is in your Heart and Feeling Center. Through your heart chakra you connect to the Divine. To reside in 5th dimensional consciousness means direct connection to the Divine within.

To live through the Divine is to have ascended. You have reached the summit. Now is the time to practice and strengthen that connection. This is your job now. Through this access point you will unwrap the many gifts that are yours to bring forward. The world needs you. Your God Self needs you. Your commitment to Source now requires that you step up.

Your responsibility is to speak your truth from within, because you are the one who undertook this mission. Thousands of us are waking up at this point so our missions can be completed. We are the groundbreakers, the lead team, the scouts who have scoured our history and our future and can report back with authority that humanity's future is Divine. All our fellow travelers must know this. This is the most critical information of our times. We must stay in alignment with our individual missions and unfold those gifts that Source bestowed upon us.

Have another conversation with your Higher Self and come back to this book as often as you need. Your Higher Self is the way you can refill your cup with promise, a promise made to us all.

God is here for you now, as has always been the case. You can visit often and fill your cup to overflowing. This is your journey.

Dr. Maurice Turmel

Message From the Ethereal

Greetings friends and neighbors. How are you? We of the ethereal realms wish to congratulate you on your efforts at finding your way Home. We can see many of you opening up now, connecting to that Divine fire within. How does it feel? Like a warm glow is it not? Suppose we suggested that you extinguish this fire, would you do so? Of course not! Why would a child of God extinguish the Light that burns so brightly within? Yet, many fellow humans show no Light at all. Have you noticed this? What can be done?

Once upon a time there was a Great Creator who sent forth emissaries to be witness to a grand design on the earth plane. These emissaries were to take the light, truth and knowledge of the Creator into their hearts and spread it among the people of the earth. The Creator wanted them to light the Lights of those who had slipped into a slumber from which they currently couldn't awaken. This Army of Light was assigned this task because the Creator knew they were ready to do the work. And in so doing, they would advance their own growth as well.

Go forth my brave ones and light the Lights of all those who have fallen asleep. They need your help and you need this experience. You see, there are many Lights to light in this world. This assignment is only a beginning. There are many dark and uncharted regions for you to explore and then illuminate. We are assembling an army of Lightworkers to pave the way for mankind. The human race is at a threshold, ready to embark on a journey that will bring them closer to Source. Their inner fire must first be reactivated. Your task is to bring this about.

First, let us determine what will be required. Lightworkers have need of three things: first, their Light must shine brightly from the Divine fire within; second, a love of life, which is where all must begin; third, the help of all humanity to achieve their ends.

The Great Creator pointed out that all Lightworkers require an audience, a state of receptivity that will benefit from their applied efforts. Without this state, the Lightworker's talents would just go to waste. Their efforts to help others would be for naught. Without a "them" there is no "you." You exist through them, and they through you. What you do for them enhances you, and what you do for yourself enhances all. Because you are of the Divine who dwells in all, your efforts will be well served. Whenever a dimmed light is reactivated, the Creator is there to cheer them on because each light that comes alive enhances all.

You see, friends, your efforts at helping yourselves and others are quite illustrious to say the least. To play a part in enhancing the growth of your Creator is no small feat. This is a most noble task. That task is to have the Divine Light awaken in the Heart of every individual on planet Earth. There are many who refuse the Light, but we see a spreading of this Light from one Soul to the next until all Light is activated and no one remains in the dark. We see this because we have seen it before. This is an acceleration of the pulse. Once that fire is lit, it leaps from Soul to Soul. Before long, all are aware that they have God residing within.

We call this "graduation" when a majority of you achieve this exalted state. You can help by lighting your own Light as brightly as you can, and by sharing what you've learned about that accomplishment. Those that need your lessons will be attracted to you. They will come because you hold a special quality that radiates the Light. When looking at you they will see a reflection of themselves. They will identify their own tiny spark as it struggles to grow. They will reach for this experience hungrily, as a person who has been without food for days. They will immediately realize this is the nourishment they've been craving. They have been missing that part of themselves for eons already, since the Big Sleep came over them so long ago.

When the Big Sleep occurred, the great clouding of the Light took hold. This happened when self-appointed leaders started fighting amongst themselves over who was right. Your world's religions stepped into the breach clamoring for attention and competing with each other for converts. It became a game. Who could win the most Souls? The orchestrators of these religions did not realize that for the Creator, whose Light burns the brightest, such competitions were meaningless. The Light of those awakening was of the Creator. So this great contest for Souls, which has carried on into the present, has been for naught. There is only one thing to be won in this life, and that is the Creator's everlasting Light and Love residing within all that lives.

Yes, Lightworkers are waking up everywhere. This is a spiritual army, the Army of Light destined to move the Earth through a process of Ascension into 5th dimensional consciousness and beyond. How does this story end, this tale of the Light? Do we take you on another flight to show you the current situation again? Or, will it suffice for us to remind you that you are here for a purpose in which you agreed to participate?

It's time to awaken, fellow travelers. It's time to come forward and show the world of what you are made. It's time to show all of creation that you are ready for service. "Where would I start?" is your only question now.

We of the ethereal realms are here to advise, not to admonish or criticize. We are here to assist with this Grand Awakening by providing a wake-up call. Are you ready to receive and extend the Light that is the legitimate source of All-That-Is? Say "yes," and your next step is before you. All of creation will be there waiting as you activate your light. When you follow the God within you will be able to turn that Light into a beacon for others to emulate.

Can you see how it goes, this spreading of the Light? It leaps from one Soul to another in the twinkling of an eye. It jumps across vast voids to brighten the whole world.

27 – Wrap Up and Final Word from Guidance

For most of this writing journey, the work has been an interaction between my Self, my Higher Self and my Guidance. They are the inspiration for my engaging in this process. You will know from your Heart Center what is right for you. You came to explore and sample the process of dialoguing with your inner world. You have been shown how to connect. Where you go now is entirely up to you. Stand by your commitment and let your heart lead the way.

A Final Word from Guidance

Now is the time to say goodbye to all of you who have been travelling this path. You have come to us with arms wide open and a willingness to learn. We have greeted you with stories as old as time itself. We have shown you that there are trials and tribulations destined to mark you for life.

Each of you has undertaken these challenges with the full understanding that better times lie ahead. Ascension and true connection have been made available. You are in the service of the Divine; your Higher Self leads the way from this point forward.

Your God Self is your Self, capital "S" Self. Your guidance is your Heart, capital "H" Heart. Your Divine inheritance has been at work behind every step you've taken. By listening to these promptings, your journey has been easier. Early resistance delivered pain. Dialoguing with your inner world has helped release that pain. Whether it was an easy ride, or one filled with conflict, it no longer matters. You have all arrived at the summit by a variety of circuitous routes, but the view from the top is the same.

You have been waiting a long time for this journey of trials to conclude. We can only advise that it had to happen in conjunction with other matters not necessarily visible to you at the time. Those of you who study Crop Circles have seen "messages in the fields." Those of you who favor the Mayan calendar know that dates such as December 21, 2012 have signaled new beginnings and the arrival of this new era. Those of you observing the Sun have been witness to its many changes and the new energies its convulsive activity continues to send our way. Multiple scenarios and multiple events have been forecasting the culmination of all these changes as a shift in consciousness from the 3rd to the 5th dimension. Internally, you have been feeling them at a core level.

It is no accident that you came to Earth at this particular time. It is no mistake or coincidence. You signed on for this and you will remember that commitment soon enough.

We have provided this service for all of you and continue providing support. We are your guides and we all worked this plan together prior to your arrival on this plane. You have been guided, steered and nudged. You have been coached into seeing things differently. You have been exposed to challenging earthly circumstances and you have all risen to meet that demand. You are strong and clear at this point, perhaps because of those obstacles. This has been your education.

School House Earth is a tough place to be, but well worth the demands in the end. You will soon see the depth and breadth of what you have gained. When you do, celebrate! Let these triumphs settle into your heart and psyche. That's how heroes and heroines are reborn.

On the hero path, the return voyage is always the easiest. The beacon guiding you Home is now visible. There will be no more groping in the dark and fumbling around for that next opening. That door is in front of you now and offers the most direct route Home, a route via your heart and feeling center.

This has been a great battle and you won. You have opened your heart and cleared out the debris. Heroines and heroes know when to leave a battle scene. They know that an enemy does not have to be crushed. That is fear's perspective. Heroes and heroines walk away as soon as that enemy is displayed for what it is – a series of faulty beliefs based on manufactured and grossly skewed information. The truth has set you free.

A simple and straightforward Ascension training program has been delivered in this book through described journaling exercises. Repeating these will take you deeper into the heart-felt experience of Ascension. This is the last hoorah for 3rd dimensional thinking. That dimension simply cannot survive your Ascension. The 5th dimension of consciousness has its own set of goals and requirements. It will no longer be undermined with 3rd dimensional struggles.

This new realm of 5th dimensional consciousness is filled with creative possibilities, endeavors that will astound you. Some possibilities include curing diseases; developing new technologies; uncovering and solving old mysteries; and, finding the remnants of ancient civilizations that once employed the tools of Conscious Evolution and connecting with Source.

Once again, the access point for all knowledge and creative energy is your heart center, your personal connection to the Divine. You will be inspired to reach for greater heights and take on tougher challenges, all leading to tremendous growth for your incarnate Self. This creative force will flow freely for all of you ready to step up.

All these changes that are now coming about are exciting. The old world of competition and domination is about to give way to cooperation between nations and individuals. What else can happen when we finally realize that we are all God incarnate?

The West is waking up to this new reality which will outshine any of its previous achievements and technological developments. Old technologies that were subordinated and crushed by 3rd dimensional power mongers will be resurrected. Tesla's late 19th century design of cheap and easily distributed electrical energy systems stands as an example. Humanity's goal will no longer be simple profit for the sake of greed. New and old creations will be allowed to flourish for the greater good.

This greater good benefits everyone and will bring more joy than anything witnessed thus far. Hunger will be a thing of the past. All will be motivated to step up and participate. Self-centeredness, rather than "Self," will also be a thing of the past. Personality cults will lose their appeal along with so many other distractions created by egos to serve other egos.

Egos are being superseded by the Self which governs your entire entity of mind, body and spirit. Self and Soul will now be your two best friends. There are still challenges ahead. By the time this shift occurs, those difficulties will be dealt with by solutions created in 5th dimensional consciousness. The 5th dimension will be the leading edge of human evolution. Scores of seekers will be waking up to this new reality and showing others how to get there, one light activating another, leaping from Soul to Soul, nation to nation and yes, world to world.

You have many cousins, psychologically speaking, on other worlds who are ready to communicate with you as soon as you shed the last vestiges of ego-centrism. Conscious self-direction is the key to advancing all life on this Earth and is a fundamental requirement before you can join similar communities scattered across the Universe. That's why we call this book Conscious Evolution, a process driven by your choices at every stage of your personal growth.

In conclusion, we want to say "Thank You" for joining us on this marvelous journey. Thank you for opening your hearts to the Divine within. Thank you for capitalizing on all those opportunities presented along the way to spur your personal development. You are wonderful students. There's much more to learn, but that will take a different turn now and there will be many new books and programs coming forth to chart the way. The main difference from where you are now will be your connection to the Divine working in tandem with ever unfolding new developments.

God is who you are. It is your Divine aspect. The end of 3rd dimensional thinking and decision making is here. Ascension into the 5th dimension is making its way around the world and following its prescribed course. A new crop of enlightened humans is ready graduate.

That's all for now, dear students. Spiritual High School is over. You will now be moving on to Graduate School where your various specialties are to be developed and ushered into the mix. Those of you, who have already progressed to this point, just keep on going. Those of you arriving at that doorstep - be prepared for a new and exciting chapter in your lives.

Thank you all for joining us on this mission. Your commitment and zeal have been noted. Journal on what you have learned here and see what your heart wants to do next.

This has been Mythology in Action. You are where you need to be.

Bonus Chapters from *The Voice*

My fellow travelers,

Once in a while you are awakened to new insights that shake up your status quo. You get so rattled your whole world goes topsy-turvy.

Is this a bad thing? No, not at all! Is it a good thing? By all means, yes! How else can you get a good night's sleep unless you are tired? How else can you wake up to new realities unless your old world view is shattered?

Positive disintegration is what this is, a chance at a new start. A world view changes as you are ready to receive the new. It unfolds through you. All life does this.

It's your reality after all that needs awakening, not mine! Ascension is clear. From where I stand I can see you there trying your hardest. But you are stumbling all over the place. There's no truth anymore to the old world order. It has to die. That's how a new age is born. The old goes first, because it doesn't work anymore. It fails to meet your needs.

It's beyond you to comprehend this fully, but it's true nevertheless. Old world orders disappear all the time. Your world history holds many examples of this.

In this book, we are examining such prospects. We are viewing change from a unique point of view, as something happening in fantasy land, but it is actually happening to you as we speak.

You are living this dream as I have described it. You are witnessing for yourselves the power of change. Old world orders come and go, as you please, but certain constants remain the same.

I am that constant in your lives, aren't I? I am the one who persists after each world order collapses and disappears. Here's a chance to do that again. The predictable leaves you wanting. The uncertain leaves you scared. Yet going to uncertainty is where you go all the time. Again, history repeats itself. You keep moving forward regardless of what's around you.

Sure, there's a lot of resistance to this process. There always is. Those who imbue the old world order with a truth they believe is unchallengeable are those who suffer the most. Because they are tied to the old, they fear the future.

The future, however, matters too. It wants to be born anew. It wants to thrive. It wants others to notice that it is available too. Where? Right in front of you, as new possibilities, potentials and reasons to move ahead.

Can you imagine not doing so? I can't. This is truth to Me. It exists because I believe in it as I've believed before. Have you not heard this mantra? "Go forward and be brave!"

Well, here it is again. Time to get going, you see. Time to unfold the new and move up to the 5th dimension of consciousness. Leave 3rd dimensional density consciousness behind, it is done for now. Time to march toward these newer possibilities.

That's how it feels from up here. I want this to happen. I need this to happen. You are My source and My inspiration. I am ready for you to come home again.

Return to Me and show Me what you've learned. I'll be glad for that purpose of yours, as I always am. We put it together, you and I, remember? Yes we did! Now you are here waiting for Me to come forward, when I am waiting for you to open. It's up to you now, you see. It is you who must open to Me, because I live inside of you and unfold through you, and your conscious choosing is necessary for me to arise.

I live in you and you are awakening. It's a good thing this purpose of ours. A real good thing! Let's get cracking and get this show on the road. It's time for this New Age to begin!

The Voice

Chapter 1 – Starmaiden

Our story begins in a lovely country setting, where there lived a young woman who was quite beautiful and charming. She had no end of suitors coming into her life, but she always felt compelled to turn them away. Something inside told her that romance was not appropriate for her at this time, and that a special angel would be coming to deliver a very important message.

Late one evening, while peering out her bedroom window, our young woman saw what appeared to be a shooting star fall across the distant sky; its tail was all ablaze, lighting a shimmering path as it crossed the horizon. Immediately, our young woman felt that her angel was at hand.

Early the next day, she rode out on her horse in the direction where she had seen the star fall. There, up ahead, in a meadow, she saw a strange sight. It was not the trail of damage one might have expected to find from a meteorite coming to Earth, but a gleaming ship of a type she had never seen before. This space vehicle was adorned with all manner of lights, blinking and glowing, as if to say it was alive. "It was a sailing ship," she thought, "but one designed to travel to and from the stars, I suppose."

Our young woman was completely captivated with its appearance. Feeling no fear, she walked around the craft a few times, examining it from every possible angle. There appeared to be no opening with which to access the interior, yet somehow she sensed there was someone aboard.

She knocked on the hull a few times to see what would happen. All of a sudden a hatch, which previously she had not noticed, opened up. Out stepped a tall, majestic looking man, dressed in white and emitting a faint glow all about him. At first glance, he did appear to be human, yet he exhibited some unusual characteristics. He did not appear to notice her, yet he seemed to be looking right through her. He stood there for a few moments, looking about the meadow, apparently drinking in every detail of

Conscious Evolution

the surrounding scenery. Turning his attention to her now, he seemed to absorb every characteristic of this lovely creature as she stood before him.

Without uttering a word, he asked her who she was. And before she could even think about a reply, in her mind, she answered "Genie."

"Then you are the special woman I've been looking for" he went on, again telepathically.

"I am?" Genie repeated this time out loud.

"Yes, you are," he stated determinedly, and then proceeded to step away from his ship to get a better view of the landscape stretching out before him.

"Where am I?" he asked as he continued to look about.

"Why you are on Earth," Genie responded, unsure as to what to say really.

"Earth, this I know," he exclaimed. "What is the name of this location here on Earth?" he continued.

"Oh, I see" Genie replied. "What is this particular area called, is what you want to know?"

"That is correct" he acknowledged.

"Well," she went on, "this is my home area here on planet Earth. It is called Lapis Land, home of the Mighty and Sweet."

"Indeed" he muttered. "Tell me then, why are you here with me now?"

"Well," Genie hesitated, "I saw a falling star last night and traced its descent to this area. This morning I decided to ride out here and see if I could find any evidence of its landing."

"I understand that," he reflected. "But, what in fact brought you to this location?"

"Oh, I see. You want to know if I felt some other form of attraction to this location, and was perhaps drawn here for reasons other than just pursuing a falling star."

"Go on" he stated.

"In all honesty, I really don't know" Genie paused. "I used to think that I would only follow my instincts if they made sense. But somehow, there seemed to be more going on this time. I just felt a need to be here and to touch this ship of yours. There was really no doubt or hesitation on my part. I just felt I had to be here."

"Good then! We understand each other" he stated flatly.

"We do?" Genie repeated, somewhat incredulously.

He looked at her and then turned away, still captivated, it seemed by the glorious landscape that spread out before him.

"This is a beautiful country" he said as he continued drinking in every scene and attuning himself to the accompanying sounds. "Breathtaking," he added. "Very magical!"

Genie just watched and listened as her companion carried on admiring everything he saw and heard.

"Tell me, dear woman" he began again, "have you ever traveled to the stars?"

"Why yes, or no," she replied hesitantly. "By yes I mean in my imagination. By no, I mean not literally."

"What is literally?" he asked.

"Oh, I mean physically" she explained, "like on a ship such as yours."

She was feeling rather anxious now. This man continued to probe her for answers to very private thoughts that she had never shared with anyone.

"I am trying to learn about you," he continued, obviously reading her thoughts again, "and I am wondering what kind of magic you might weave?"

"Magic?" she repeated.

"Yes, magic," he went on. "In my home area, women are weavers of magic, capable of spinning many fantastic ideas and yarns. Not the kind from which you make clothes mind you, but the kind you tell stories with."

"Oh, yarns, yes," Genie now understood. "Yes I do weave yarns sometimes to amuse myself, or to entertain children and teach a lesson or two."

"Good," he said, "then you will be very useful on our journey together."

"I will?" she repeated.

"Of course! Of what value would you be if you could not weave tales? Your world has need of stories to help its occupants find their way. They are lost and asleep and conventional methods of instruction have failed to serve them in their quest for truth. They have need of yarns, beautiful magical tales, that can transport them out of themselves into a world of fantasy and magic, where they can perceive themselves from a different point of view."

Now Genie was aghast.

"You expect me to do all this?" she asked, feeling rather bewildered.

"Yes, I do," he replied. "For I am Stargazer and you are Starmaiden, and we have come together at this time to prepare you for instructing this race of people."

"But, these are my people" she protested. "I am one of them. Why are you saying these things to me?"

She was quite anxious now, wondering where all of this was going.

"A long time ago, when you were quite young," he began again, "I visited you one night. I whispered to you softly and told you who you were and why you were here on this Earth.

I explained to you that I would return at a later time and the two of us would set off together on a very important journey. But first, you had to grow up in this environment and learn the customs of these people. Once that was accomplished, you would be ready for the challenges ahead."

"I see," Genie stated as she sat down to absorb all of what she just heard. "When I was younger I do remember being visited by a stranger who told me such things. This is coming back to me now. And he said he would return for me at a future time. That was you?" she asked, looking straight at him with a glint of recognition spreading across her face.

"That was I, dear woman. That was I," he repeated for emphasis.

"But I don't understand," she went on. "How could I forget all that and yet, still hear you in my head and know that what you say is true? I find this very confusing."

"Understandably so," he went on. "When you were young, you were open to magic and mystery. The universe, the stars, all manner of life intrigued you. As you grew older, this material world pressed itself upon you and you forgot many of the teachings that were given to you at the beginning of this venture. These teachings were embedded into your cellular memory so as to never be lost. But your consciousness did lose sight of them. These will reawaken again, as we proceed on this journey together. Each step of the way, important facets of these earlier instructions will come back to you, and you will know that they are true because of the feelings in your heart."

"In my heart?" she repeated, covering her chest with her hand.

"Yes, in your heart" he repeated, "where all such truths are written. The Great Creator has written these truths in all of our hearts, to be found and recovered, at key points in our lives."

"But, how is this to happen for me?" she wanted to know. "How will I find my truths?"

"By your own feelings will you know them," he proceeded to explain. "And by the reactions your whole body will show to any situation or event."

"Like I'm having right now, with your words?" she asked.

"That is correct. In this feeling state, you will know all such truths, as they will show an unmistakable marking to you in the form of a vibration. That vibration is a key to your personal knowledge. Each time that key, or vibration, is activated, you will have discovered some new and important information about yourself that will be undeniable. Do you have any further questions before we proceed?" he added.

"No, not at the moment" she answered. "But I do wish to know how I can go off with you and not say something to my family. They will be concerned about me and will want to know the details of who you are."

Stargazer pondered her reaction for a moment, and then offered this reply.

"Let them know that you have awakened to a new reality, that a quest has been thrust upon you, and that you must pursue it. This they will understand, as do all who have parented a very special being. They will release you to your tasks. Do not be concerned about that."

"Very well," Genie answered. "I will go to my home and tell my parents what I must do. Then I will return to you here tomorrow, to begin this journey together."

"Do you understand what this is all about?" Stargazer asked again.

"I only understand that I must go with you. I have been waiting for this for some time it seems. Now that you are here, it is time for me to proceed. This is all I know at the moment."

Genie then rode off in the direction of her home as Stargazer set about to camp for the night. He knew in his heart that he had come to the right place. He knew this for certain as soon as he saw Starmaiden standing before him. She was truly special, much as he had envisioned her to be, not at all like the child he had met so long ago. With that thought in mind he sat down to contemplate. He would go into a meditative state, where he could consult with the members of his army of thieves. They were not real thieves, but mischievous guides as they liked to be referred to, in keeping with their unpredictable ways.

As Stargazer sat down beside the ship, he imagined how life would be 1,000 years from this time, when travelers of all sorts would be wandering about the universe, sharing, cavorting, and telling each other their yarns. Yes, it would be an amazing place, this Earth. But again, it was always amazing this mystery called Life. "Till that unknown future then," and he drifted into a meditative trance, to travel as it were, wherever his mind and guidance might take him. Who knew for sure? Only the journey itself would tell the tale.

You can purchase The Voice and continue your journey at http://www.wordbranch.com/the-voice.html

For a limited time, you can get 10% off any Word Branch Publishing book purchased from the WBP book store. Enter the code CD10 at checkout.

About the Author

 Maurice Turmel PhD, AKA "Dr Moe," is a retired psychologist with over four decades of experience in personal growth and the helping professions. Those early years of personal growth pursuits were then coupled with traditional psychological training which led to his growing passion for a deeper understanding of the spiritual and mythological foundations of modern psychology. Today, Dr Moe describes himself as a Spiritual Psychologist, integrating traditional psychology with New Thought spiritual practices in order to provide a clearer picture of who we are as a divinely sourced human species. Dr Moe's writings include inspirational short stories and poetry in an early collection titled "Mythical Times," a spiritual sci-fi novel: "The Voice;" a non-fiction follow-up to the novel: "Conscious Evolution;" and a healing book of short stories, poetry, reflections and coping strategies titled: "How to Cope with Grief and Loss."

Dr Moe is also an avid songwriter with dozens of compositions reflecting the same themes as those addressed in his books.

His musical compositions and several Grief & Loss related videos are available on YouTube:
http://www.youtube.com/user/drmoe2000/videos

Also written by Dr. Maurice Turmel:
The Voice: A Mythological Guide to Mankind's Ascension:
http://www.wordbranch.com/the-voice.html
Coping with Grief and Loss: http://www.wordbranch.com/coping-with-grief.html

You may also like:
The Lost Art of Loving by Johanna Carroll:
http://www.wordbranch.com/store/p13/The_Lost_Art_of_Loving.html
Feel Your Soul by Ieva Salina:
http://www.wordbranch.com/store/p31/Feel_Your_Soul.html

You can purchase Dr. Tumel's books at: http://wordbranch.com

You can email the author with your questions and comments at dr.moe@wordbranch.com.

If you liked *Conscious Evolution*, please leave feedback.

Conscious Evolution is published by Word Branch Publishing, an independent publisher located in Marble, North Carolina. If you have a finished, or near-finished, book, we would like to hear about it. Word Branch Publishing believes that everyone has something important to say. http://wordbranch.com

Word Branch Publishing:
Independent Publishing for Independent Readers.

See more of Word Branch Publishing's books at
http://wordbranch.com/book-shop.html

www.ingramcontent.com/pod-product-compliance
Lightning Source LLC
LaVergne TN
LVHW051229080426
835513LV00016B/1487